Penguin Books
The Book of Imaginary Beings

Jorge Luis Borges was born in Buenos Aires in 1899
and was educated in Europe. One of the major
writers of our time, he has published many
collections of poems, essays, and short stories. In
1961, Borges shared the International Publishers'
Prize with Samuel Beckett. The Ingram Merrill
Foundation granted him its Annual Literary Award
in 1966 for his 'outstanding contribution to
literature'. In 1970 he was awarded the degree of
Doctor of Letters, *honoris causa*, from both Columbia
and Oxford, and in 1971 won the fifth biennial
Jerusalem Prize, being awarded the Alfonso Reyes
Prize in 1973. *Time* has called him 'the greatest
living writer in the Spanish language today', while
the *New York Herald Tribune* has described him as
'unquestionably the most brilliant South American
writing today'. He is former Director of the
Argentine National Library. *A Universal History of
Infamy, Labyrinths, Doctor Brodie's Report* and *The
Book of Sand* are also published in Penguins.

Norman Thomas di Giovanni is an American now
living in Scotland. He worked with Borges in Buenos
Aires from 1968 to 1972, and, to date, has produced
eight volumes of Borges's verse and prose in English.

D1334859

Jorge Luis Borges

with *Margarita Guerrero*

The Book of Imaginary Beings

Revised, enlarged and translated by
Norman Thomas di Giovanni
in collaboration with the author

Penguin Books

Penguin Books Ltd, Harmondsworth,
Middlesex, England
Penguin Books, 625 Madison Avenue,
New York, New York 10022, U.S.A.
Penguin Books Australia Ltd, Ringwood,
Victoria, Australia
Penguin Books Canada Ltd,
2801 John Street, Markham, Ontario, Canada L3R 1B4
Penguin Books (N.Z.) Ltd,
182–190 Wairau Road, Auckland 10, New Zealand

El libro de los seres imaginarios
First published in Buenos Aires 1967
Translation published in the U.S.A. 1969

First published in Great Britain by Jonathan Cape 1970
Published in Penguin Books 1974
Reprinted with revisions 1974
Reprinted 1980

Set, printed and bound in Great Britain by
Cox & Wyman Ltd, Reading
Set in Linotype Pilgrim

Grateful acknowledgement is made for permission to reprint the following material:

'An Animal Imagined by Kafka', reprinted by permission of Schocken Books Inc., from *Dearest Father* by Franz Kafka, © 1954 by Schocken Books Inc.

'An Animal Imagined by C. S. Lewis' and 'A Creature Imagined by C. S. Lewis', reprinted by permission of C. S. Lewis, from *Perelandra*, © 1947 by C. S. Lewis. Published by The Macmillan Company, New York, and The Bodley Head, London.

'A Crossbreed', reprinted by permission of Shocken Books Inc., from *Description of a Struggle* by Franz Kafka, © 1946, 1958 by Schocken Books Inc.

'The Odradek', reprinted by permission of Schocken Books Inc., from *The Penal Colony* by Franz Kafka, © 1948 by Schocken Books Inc.

The following pieces first appeared in the *New Yorker*, October 4th, 1969: 'A Bao A Qu', 'The Barometz', 'The Celestial Stag', 'The Chinese Dragon', 'The Elves', 'Fauna of Mirrors', 'Haniel, Kafziel, Azriel, and Aniel', 'The Hundred-Heads', 'The Leveler', 'The Lunar Hare', 'The Nymphs', 'The Pygmies', 'The Rain Bird', 'The Shaggy Beast of La Ferté-Bernard', 'The Sphinx', 'Swedenborg's Angels', 'Swedenborg's Devils', 'Thermal Beings', 'Two Metaphysical Beings', 'The Western Dragon'.

Contents

Preface

As we all know, there is a kind of lazy pleasure in useless and out-of-the-way erudition. The compilation and translation of this volume have given us a great deal of such pleasure; we hope the reader will share something of the fun we felt when ransacking the bookshelves of our friends and the mazelike vaults of the Biblioteca Nacional in search of old authors and abstruse references. We have done our best to trace all our quoted material back to original sources and to translate it from the original tongues — medieval Latin, French, German, Italian, and Spanish. Lemprière and the Loeb and Bohn collections have, as is their wont, proved most helpful with the classics. As for our invincible ignorance of Eastern languages, it enables us to be grateful for the labours of such men as Giles, Burton, Lane, Waley, and Scholem.

The first edition of this book, containing eighty-two pieces, was published in Mexico in 1957. It was called then *Manual de zoología fantástica* (Handbook of Fantastic Zoology). In 1967, a second edition — *El libro de los seres imaginarios* — was published in Buenos Aires with thirty-four additional articles. Now, for this English-language edition, we have altered a good number of the original articles, correcting, adding, or revising material, and we have also compiled a few brand-new ones. This latest edition contains 120 pieces.

We extend warm thanks for their help to Marian Skedgell, of E. P. Dutton, and to José Edmundo Clemente, Assistant Director of the Argentine National Library.

Buenos Aires, 23 May 1969   J.L.B. N.T. di G.

Preface to the 1967 Edition

The title of this book would justify the inclusion of Prince Hamlet, of the point, of the line, of the surface, of n-dimensional hyperplanes and hypervolumes, of all generic terms, and perhaps of each one of us and of the godhead. In brief, the sum of all things – the universe. We have limited ourselves, however, to what is immediately suggested by the words 'imaginary beings'; we have compiled a handbook of the strange creatures conceived through time and space by the human imagination.

We are ignorant of the meaning of the dragon in the same way that we are ignorant of the meaning of the universe, but there is something in the dragon's image that fits man's imagination, and this accounts for the dragon's appearance in different places and periods.

A book of this kind is unavoidably incomplete; each new edition forms the basis of future editions, which themselves may grow on endlessly.

We invite the eventual reader in Colombia or Paraguay to send us the names, accurate description, and most conspicuous traits of their local monsters.

As with all miscellanies, as with the inexhaustible volumes of Robert Burton, of Frazer, or of Pliny, *The Book of Imaginary Beings* is not meant to be read straight through; rather, we should like the reader to dip into these pages at random, just as one plays with the shifting patterns of a kaleidoscope.

The sources of this collection are manifold; they are recorded in each piece. May we be forgiven any accidental omission.

Martínez, September 1967   J.L.B. M.G.

Preface to the 1957 Edition

A small child is taken to the zoo for the first time. This child may be any one of us or, to put it another way, we have been this child and have forgotten about it. In these grounds – these terrible grounds – the child sees living animals he has never before glimpsed; he sees jaguars, vultures, bison, and – what is still stranger – giraffes. He sees for the first time the bewildering variety of the animal kingdom, and this spectacle, which might alarm or frighten him, he enjoys. He enjoys it so much that going to the zoo is one of the pleasures of childhood, or is thought to be such. How can we explain this everyday and yet mysterious event?

We can, of course, deny it. We can suppose that children suddenly rushed off to the zoo will become, in due time, neurotic, and the truth is there can hardly be a child who has not visited the zoo and there is hardly a grown-up who is not a neurotic. It may be stated that all children, by definition, are explorers, and that to discover the camel is in itself no stranger than to discover a mirror or water or a staircase. It can also be stated that the child trusts his parents, who take him to this place full of animals. Besides, his toy tiger and the pictures of tigers in the encyclopedia have somehow taught him to look at the flesh-and-bone tiger without fear. Plato (if he were invited to join in this discussion) would tell us that the child had already seen the tiger in a primal world of archetypes, and that now on seeing the tiger he recognizes it. Schopenhauer (even more wondrously) would tell us that the child looks at the tigers without fear because he is aware that he is the tigers and the tigers are him or, more accurately, that both he and the tigers are but forms of that single essence, the Will.

Let us pass now from the zoo of reality to the zoo of

mythologies, to the zoo whose denizens are not lions but sphinxes and griffons and centaurs. The population of this second zoo should exceed by far the population of the first, since a monster is no more than a combination of parts of real beings, and the possibilities of permutation border on the infinite. In the centaur, the horse and man are blended; in the Minotaur, the bull and man (Dante imagined it as having the face of a man and the body of a bull); and in this way it seems we could evolve an endless variety of monsters – combinations of fishes, birds, and reptiles, limited only by our own boredom or disgust. This, however, does not happen; our monsters would be stillborn, thank God. Flaubert had rounded up, in the last pages of his *Temptation of Saint Anthony*, a number of medieval and classical monsters and has tried – so say his commentators – to concoct a few new ones; his sum total is hardly impressive, and but few of them really stir our imaginations. Anyone looking into the pages of the present handbook will soon find out that the zoology of dreams is far poorer than the zoology of the Maker.

We are as ignorant of the meaning of the dragon as we are of the meaning of the universe, but there is something in the dragon's image that appeals to the human imagination, and so we find the dragon in quite distinct places and times. It is, so to speak, a necessary monster, not an ephemeral or accidental one, such as the three-headed chimera or the catoblepas.

Of course, we are fully aware that this book, perhaps the first of its kind, does not exhaust the sum total of imaginary animals. We have delved into classical and Oriental literatures, but we feel that our subject goes on for ever.

We have deliberately excluded the many legends of men taking the shapes of animals: the *lobisón*, the werewolf, and so on.

We wish to acknowledge the help given us by Leonor Guerrero de Coppola, Alberto D'Aversa, and Rafael López Pellegri.

Martínez, 29 January 1957   J.L.B. M.G.

A Bao A Qu

If you want to look out over the loveliest landscape in the world, you must climb to the top of the Tower of Victory in Chitor. There, standing on a circular terrace, one has a sweep of the whole horizon. A winding stairway gives access to this terrace, but only those who do not believe in the legend dare climb up. The tale runs:

On the stairway of the Tower of Victory there has lived since the beginning of time a being sensitive to the many shades of the human soul and known as the A Bao A Qu. It lies dormant, for the most part on the first step, until at the approach of a person some secret life is touched off in it, and deep within the creature an inner light begins to glow. At the same time, its body and almost translucent skin begin to stir. But only when someone starts up the spiralling stairs is the A Bao A Qu brought to consciousness, and then it sticks close to the visitor's heels, keeping to the outside of the turning steps, where they are most worn by the generations of pilgrims. At each level the creature's colour becomes more intense, its shape approaches perfection, and the bluish form it gives off is more brilliant. But it achieves its ultimate form only at the topmost step, when the climber is a person who has attained Nirvana and whose acts cast no shadows. Otherwise, the A Bao A Qu hangs back before reaching the top, as if paralysed, its body incomplete, its blue growing paler, and its glow hesitant. The creature suffers when it cannot come to completion, and its moan is a barely audible sound, something like the rustling of silk. Its span of life is brief, since as soon as the traveller climbs down, the A Bao A Qu wheels and tumbles to the first steps, where, worn out and almost shapeless, it waits for the next visitor. People say that its tentacles are visible only when it reaches the middle of the staircase. It is also said that it can see with its whole body and that to the touch it is like the skin of a peach.

In the course of centuries, the A Bao A Qu has reached the terrace only once.

This legend is recorded by C. C. Iturvuru in an appendix to his now classic treatise *On Malay Witchcraft* (1937).

Abtu and Anet

As all Egyptians knew, Abtu and Anet were two life-sized fishes, identical and holy, that swam on the lookout for danger before the prow of the sun god's ship. Their course was endless; by day the craft sailed the sky from east to west, from dawn to dusk, and by night made its way underground in the opposite direction.

The Amphisbaena

The *Pharsalia* (IX, 701–28) catalogues the real or imaginary reptiles that Cato's soldiers met up with on their scorching march across the African desert. Among them are the Pareas, 'content with its tail to cleave its track' (or as a seventeenth-century Spanish poet has it, 'which makes its way, erect as a staff'), and the Jaculi, which darts from trees like javelins, and 'the dangerous Amphisbaena, also, that moves on at both of its heads'. Pliny (VIII, 23) uses nearly the same words to describe the Amphisbaena, adding: 'as if she were not hurtfull enough to cast her poyson at one mouth only'. Brunetto Latini's *Tesoro* – the encyclopedia which Latini recommended to his old disciple in the seventh circle of Hell – is less terse and clearer: 'The Amphisbaena is a serpent having two heads, the one in its proper place and the other in its tail; and it can bite with both, and run with agility, and its eyes glare like candles.' Sir Thomas Browne in his *Vulgar Errors* (1646) wrote that there is no species without a bottom, top, front, back, left, and right, and he denied the existence of the Amphisbaena, 'for the senses being placed at both extreams, doth make both ends anterior, which is impossible ... And therefore this duplicity was ill contrived to place one head at both extreams ...' Amphisbaena, in Greek, means 'goes both ways'. In the Antilles and in certain parts of America, the name is given to a reptile commonly known as the *doble andadora* (Both ways goer), the 'two-headed snake', and 'mother of ants'. It is said that ants nourish it. Also that if it is chopped in half, its two parts will join again.

The Amphisbaena's medicinal properties were celebrated by Pliny.

An Animal Imagined by Kafka

It is the animal with the big tail, a tail many yards long and like a fox's brush. How I should like to get my hands on this tail some time, but it is impossible, the animal is constantly moving about, the tail is constantly being flung this way and that. The animal resembles a kangaroo, but not as to the face, which is flat almost like a human face, and small and oval; only its teeth have any power of expression, whether they are concealed or bared. Sometimes I have the feeling that the animal is trying to tame me.

What other purpose could it have in withdrawing its tail when I snatch at it, and then again waiting calmly until I am tempted again, and then leaping away once more?

FRANZ KAFKA: *Dearest Father*

(Translated from the German by
Ernst Kaiser and Eithne Wilkins)

An Animal Imagined by
C. S. Lewis

The noise was very loud now and the thicket very dense so that he could not see a yard ahead, when the music stopped suddenly. There was a sound of rustling and broken twigs and he made hastily in that direction, but found nothing. He had almost decided to give up the search when the song began again a little farther away. Once more he made after it; once more the creature stopped singing and evaded him. He must have played thus at hide-and-seek with it for the best part of an hour before his search was rewarded.

Treading delicately during one of the loudest bursts of music he at last saw through the flowery branches a black something. Standing still whenever it stopped singing, and advancing with great caution whenever it began again, he stalked it for ten minutes. At last it was in full view, and singing, and ignorant that it was watched. It sat upright like a dog, black and sleek and shiny, but its shoulders were high above Ransom's head, and the forelegs on which they were pillared were like young trees and the wide soft pads on which they rested were large as those of a camel. The enormous rounded belly was white, and far up above the shoulders the neck rose like that of a horse. The head was in profile from where Ransom stood – the mouth wide open as it sang of joy in thick-coming trills, and the music almost visibly rippled in its glossy throat. He stared in wonder at the wide liquid eyes and the quivering, sensitive nostrils. Then the creature stopped, saw him, and darted away, and stood, now a few paces distant, on all four legs, not much smaller than a young elephant, swaying a long bushy tail. It was the first thing in Perelandra which seemed to show any fear of man. Yet it was not fear. When he called to it it came nearer. It put its velvet nose into his hand and endured his touch; but almost at once it darted back and, bending its long neck, buried its head in its paws. He could make no headway with it, and when at length it retreated out of sight he did not follow it. To do so would have seemed an injury to its fawn-like shyness, to the yielding softness of its expression, its evident wish to be for ever a sound and only a sound in the thickest centre of untravelled woods. He resumed his journey: a few seconds later the song broke out behind him, louder and lovelier than before, as if in a paean of rejoicing at its recovered privacy.

'The beasts of that kind have no milk [said Perelandra] and always what they bring forth is suckled by the she-beast of another kind. She is great and beautiful and dumb, and till the young singing beast is weaned it is among her whelps and is subject to her. But when it is grown it becomes the most delicate and glorious of all beasts and goes from her. And she wonders at its song.'

C. S. LEWIS: Perelandra

The Animal Imagined by Poe

In his *Narrative of Arthur Gordon Pym of Nantucket*, published in 1838, Edgar Allan Poe attributed to certain Antarctic islands an astounding yet credible fauna. In Chapter XVIII, we read:

> We also picked up a bush, full of red berries, like those of the hawthorn, and the carcass of a singular-looking land-animal. It was three feet in length, and but six inches in height, with four very short legs, the feet armed with long claws of a brilliant scarlet, and resembling coral in substance. The body was covered with a straight silky hair, perfectly white. The tail was peaked like that of a rat, and about a foot and a half long. The head resembled a cat's, with the exception of the ears; these were flapped like the ears of a dog. The *teeth* were of the same brilliant scarlet as the claws.

No less remarkable was the water found in those southern regions. Towards the close of the chapter, Poe writes:

> On account of the singular character of the water, we refused to taste it, supposing it to be polluted . . . I am at a loss to give a distinct idea of the nature of this liquid, and cannot do so without many words. Although it flowed with rapidity in all declivities where common water would do so, yet never, except when falling in a cascade, had it the customary appearance of *limpidity*. It was, nevertheless, in point of fact, as perfectly limpid as any limestone water in existence, the difference being only in appearance. At first sight, and especially in cases where little declivity was found, it bore resemblance, as regards consistency, to a thick infusion of gum-arabic in common

water. But this was only the least remarkable of its extra-ordinary qualities. It was *not* colourless, nor was it of any one uniform colour – presenting to the eye, as it flowed, every possible shade of purple, like the hues of a change-able silk . . . Upon collecting a basinful, and allowing it to settle thoroughly, we perceived that the whole mass of liquid was made up of a number of distinct veins, each of a distinct hue; that these veins did not commingle; and that their cohesion was perfect in regard to their own particles among themselves, and imperfect in regard to neighbouring veins. Upon passing the blade of a knife ath-wart the veins, the water closed over it immediately, as with us, and also, in withdrawing it, all traces of the pass-age of the knife were instantly obliterated. If, however, the blade was passed down accurately between the two veins, a perfect separation was effected, which the power of cohesion did not immediately rectify.

Animals in the Form of Spheres

The sphere is the most uniform of solid bodies since every point on its surface is equidistant from its centre. Because of this, and because of its ability to revolve on an axis without straying from a fixed place, Plato (*Timaeus*, 33) approved the judgement of the Demiurge, who gave the world a spherical shape. Plato thought the world to be a living being and in the *Laws* (898) stated that the planets and stars were living as well. In this way, he enriched fantastic zoology with vast spherical animals and cast aspersions on those slow-witted astronomers who failed to understand that the circular course of heavenly bodies was voluntary.

In Alexandria over five hundred years later, Origen, one

of the Fathers of the Church, taught that the blessed would come back to life in the form of spheres and would enter rolling into Heaven.

During the Renaissance, the idea of Heaven as an animal reappeared in Lucilio Vanini; the Neoplatonist Marsilio Ficino spoke of the hair, teeth, and bones of the earth; and Giordano Bruno felt that the planets were great peaceful animals, warm-blooded, with regular habits, and endowed with reason. At the beginning of the seventeenth century, the German astronomer Johannes Kepler debated with the English mystic Robert Fludd which of them had first conceived the notion of the earth as a living monster, 'whose whalelike breathing, changing with sleep and wakefulness, produces the ebb and flow of the sea'. The anatomy, the feeding habits, the colour, the memory, and the imaginative and shaping faculties of the monster were sedulously studied by Kepler.

In the nineteenth century, the German psychologist Gustav Theodor Fechner (a man praised by William James in his *A Pluralistic Universe*) rethought the preceding ideas with all the earnestness of a child. Anyone not belittling his hypothesis that the earth, our mother, is an organism – an organism superior to plants, animals, and men – may look into the pious pages of Fechner's *Zend-Avesta*. There we read, for example, that the earth's spherical shape is that of the human eye, the noblest organ of our body. Also, that 'if the sky is really the home of angels, these angels are obviously the stars, for the sky has no other inhabitants'.

Antelopes with Six Legs

It is said that Odin's horse, the grey-coated Sleipnir – who travels on land, in the air, and down into the regions of Hell – is provided (or encumbered) with eight legs; a Siberian myth attributes six legs to the first Antelopes. With such an endowment it was difficult or impossible to catch them; Tunk-poj, the divine huntsman, made some special skates with the wood of a sacred tree which creaked incessantly and that the barking of a dog had revealed to him. The skates creaked too and flew with the speed of an arrow; to control or restrain their course, he found it necessary to wedge into the skates some blocks made of the wood of another magic tree. All over heaven Tunk-poj hunted the Antelope. The beast, tired out, fell to the ground, and Tunk-poj cut off its hindmost pair of legs.

'Men,' said Tunk-poj, 'grow smaller and weaker every day. How are they going to hunt six-legged Antelopes if I myself am barely able to?'

From that day on, Antelopes have been quadrupeds.

The Ass with Three Legs

Pliny attributes to Zarathustra, founder of the religion still professed by the Parsis of Bombay, the composition of two million verses; the Arab historian al-Tabari claims that Zarathustra's complete works as set down by pious calligraphers cover some twelve thousand cowhides. It is well known that Alexander of Macedonia had these parchments burned in

Persepolis, but thanks to the retentive memory of the priests, it was possible to preserve the basic texts, and from the ninth century these have been supplemented by an encyclopedic work, the *Bundahish*, which contains this page:

Of the three-legged ass it is said that it stands in the middle of the ocean and that three is the number of its hooves and six the number of its eyes and nine the number of its mouths and two the number of its ears and one the number of its horn. Its coat is white, its food is spiritual, and its whole being is righteous. And two of its six eyes are in the place where eyes should be and two on the crown of its head and two in its forehead; through the keenness of its six eyes it triumphs and destroys.

Of its nine mouths, three are placed in the face and three in the forehead and three on the inside of its loins . . . Each hoof, laid on the ground, covers the space of a flock of a thousand sheep, and under each of its spurs up to a thousand horsemen can manoeuvre. As to its ears, they overshadow [the north Persian province of] Mazanderan. Its horn is as of gold and is hollow, and from it a thousand branchlets have grown. With this horn will it bring down and scatter all the machinations of the wicked.

Amber is known to be the dung of the three-legged ass. In the mythology of Mazdaism, this beneficent monster is one of the helpers of Ahura Mazdah (Ormuzd), the principle of Life, Light, and Truth.

Bahamut

Behemoth's fame reached the wastes of Arabia, where men altered and magnified its image. From a hippopotamus or elephant they turned it into a fish afloat in a fathomless sea; on the fish they placed a bull, and on the bull a ruby mountain, and on the mountain an angel, and over the angel six hells, and over these hells the earth, and over the earth seven heavens. A Moslem tradition runs:

> God made the earth, but the earth had no base and so under the earth he made an angel. But the angel had no base and so under the angel's feet he made a crag of ruby. But the crag had no base and so under the crag he made a bull endowed with four thousand eyes, ears, nostrils, mouths, tongues and feet. But the bull had no base and so under the bull he made a fish named Bahamut, and under the fish he put water, and under the water he put darkness, and beyond this men's knowledge does not reach.

Others have it that the earth has its foundation on the water; the water, on the crag; the crag, on the bull's forehead; the bull, on a bed of sand; the sand, on Bahamut; Bahamut, on a stifling wind; the stifling wind on a mist. What lies under the mist is unknown.

So immense and dazzling is Bahamut that the eyes of man cannot bear its sight. All the seas of the world, placed in one of the fish's nostrils, would be like a mustard seed laid in the desert. In the 496th night of the *Arabian Nights* we are told that it was given to Isa (Jesus) to behold Bahamut and that, this mercy granted, Isa fell to the ground in a faint, and three days and their nights passed before he recovered his senses. The tale goes on that beneath the measureless fish is a sea; and beneath the sea, a chasm of air; and beneath the air, fire; and beneath the fire, a serpent named Falak in whose mouth are the six hells.

The idea of the crag resting on the bull, and the bull on Bahamut, and Bahamut on anything else, seems to be an illustration of the cosmological proof of the existence of God. This proof argues that every cause requires a prior cause, and so, in order to avoid proceeding into infinity, a first cause is necessary.

Baldanders

Baldanders (whose name we may translate as *Soon-another* or *At-any-moment-something-else*) was suggested to the master shoemaker Hans Sachs (1494–1576) of Nuremburg by that passage in the *Odyssey* in which Menelaus pursues the Egyptian god Proteus, who changes himself into a lion, a serpent, a panther, a huge wild boar, a tree, and flowing water. Some ninety years after Sachs's death, Baldanders makes a new appearance in the last book of the picaresque-fantastic novel by Grimmelshausen, *The Adventuresome Simplicissimus* (1669). In the midst of a wood, the hero comes upon a stone statue which seems to him an idol from some old Germanic temple. He touches it and the statue tells him he is Baldanders and thereupon takes the forms of a man, of an oak tree, of a sow, of a fat sausage, of a field of clover, of dung, of a flower, of a blossoming branch, of a mulberry bush, of a silk tapestry, of many other things and beings, and then, once more, of a man. He pretends to teach Simplicissimus the art 'of conversing with things which by their nature are dumb, such as chairs and benches, pots and pans'; he also makes himself into a secretary and writes these words from the Revelation of St John: 'I am the first and the last', which are the key to the coded document in which he leaves the hero his instructions. Baldanders adds that his emblem (like that of the Turk, and with more right to it than the Turk) is the inconstant moon.

Baldanders is a successive monster, a monster in time. The title page of the first edition of Grimmelshausen's novel takes up the joke. It bears an engraving of a creature having a satyr's head, a human torso, the unfolded wings of a bird, and the tail of a fish, and which, with a goat's leg and vulture's claws, tramples on a heap of masks that stand for the succession of shapes he has taken. In his belt he carries a sword and in his hands an open book showing pictures of a crown, a sailing boat, a goblet, a tower, a child, a pair of dice, a fool's cap with bells, and a piece of ordnance.

The Banshee

Nobody seems to have laid eyes on this 'woman of the fairies'. She is less a shape than a mournful screaming that haunts the Irish night and (according to Sir Walter Scott's *Demonology and Witchcraft*) the Scottish highlands. Beneath the windows of the visited house, she foretells the death of one of the family. She is held to be a token of pure Celtic blood, with no mixture of Latin, Saxon, or Danish. The Banshee has also been heard in Wales and in Brittany. Her wail is called keening.

The Barometz

The vegetable Lamb of Tartary, also named Barometz and *Lycopodium barometz* and Chinese lycopodium, is a plant whose shape is that of a lamb bearing a golden fleece. It stands on four or five root stalks. Sir Thomas Browne gives this description of it in his *Pseudodoxia Epidemica* (1646):

> Much wonder is made of the Baromez, that strange plant-animal or vegetable Lamb of *Tartary*, which Wolves delight to feed on, which hath the shape of a Lamb, affordeth a bloody juyce upon breaking, and liveth while the plants be consumed about it.

Other monsters are made up by combining various kinds of animals; the Barometz is a union of animal and vegetable kingdoms.

This brings to mind the mandrake, which cries out like a man when it is ripped from the earth; and in one of the circles of the *Inferno*, the sad forest of the suicides, from whose torn limbs blood and words drip at the same time; and that tree dreamed by Chesterton, which devoured the birds nesting in its branches, and when spring came put out feathers instead of leaves.

The Basilisk

Down through the ages, the Basilisk (also known as the Cockatrice) grows increasingly ugly and horrendous until today it is forgotten. Its name comes from the Greek and means 'little king'; to the Elder Pliny (VIII, 21), it was a serpent bearing 'a white spot like a starre ... on the head, and sets it out like a coronet or diadem'. Dating from the Middle Ages, it becomes a four-legged cock with a crown, yellow feathers, wide thorny wings, and a serpent's tail ending either in a hook or in another cock's head. The change in its image is reflected in a change in its name; Chaucer in 'The Persone's Tale' speaks of the 'basilicok' ('the basilicok sleeth folk by the venim of his sighte'). One of the plates illustrating Aldrovandi's *Natural History of Serpents and Dragons* gives the Basilisk scales instead of feathers, and the use of eight legs. (According to the Younger Edda, Odin's horse Sleipnir also had eight legs.)

What remains constant about the Basilisk is the deadly effect of its stare and its venom. The Gorgons' eyes turned living beings into stone; Lucan tells us that from the blood of one of them all the serpents of Libya sprang – the asp, the amphisbaena, the ammodyte, and the Basilisk. We give the following passages, in a literal translation, from Book IX of *Pharsalia*:

> In this body [Medusa's] first did noxious nature produce deadly plagues; from those jaws snakes poured forth whizzing hisses with vibrating tongues, which, after the manner of a woman's hair flowing along the back, flapped about the very neck of the delighted Medusa. Upon her forehead turned towards you erect did serpents rise, and viper's venom flowed from her combed locks.

> What avails a Basilisk being pierced by the spear of the wretched Murrus? Swift flies the poison along the weapon, and fastens upon the hand; which, instantly, with sword unsheathed, he smites, and at the same moment severs it entirely from the arm; and, looking upon the dreadful warning of a death his own, he stands in safety, his hand perishing.

The Basilisk dwelled in the desert; or, more accurately, it

made the desert. Birds fell dead at its feet and the earth's fruits blackened and rotted; the water of the streams where it quenched its thirst remained poisoned for centuries. That its mere glance split rocks and burned grass has been attested by Pliny. Of all animals, the weasel alone was unaffected by the monster and could be counted on to attack it on sight; it was also believed that the crowing of a rooster sent the Basilisk scurrying. The seasoned traveller was careful to provide himself with either a caged rooster or a weasel before venturing into unknown territory. Another weapon was the mirror; its own image would strike the Basilisk dead.

Isidore of Seville and the compilers of the *Speculum Triplex* (Threefold Mirror) rejected Lucan's fables and sought a rational explanation for the Basilisk's origin. (They could not deny its existence, since the Vulgate translates the Hebrew word *Tsepha*, the name of a poisonous reptile, as 'cockatrice'.) The theory that gained most favour was that of a misshapen egg laid by a cock and hatched by a snake or a toad. In the seventeenth century, Sir Thomas Browne found this explanation as farfetched as the monster itself. At much the same time, Quevedo wrote his *romance* 'The Basilisk', in which we read:

> Si está vivo quien te vio,
> Toda su historia es mentira,
> Pues si no murió, te ignora,
> Y si murió no lo afirma.

> [If the man who saw you is still alive, your whole story is a lie, since if he has not died he cannot have seen you, and if he has died, he cannot tell what he saw.]

Behemoth

Four centuries before the Christian era, Behemoth was a magnification of the elephant or of the hippopotamus, or a mistaken and alarmist version of these animals; it is now – precisely – the ten famous verses describing it in Job (XL: 15–24) and the huge being which these lines evoke. The rest is wrangling and philology.

The word 'Behemoth' is plural; scholars tell us it is the intensive plural form of the Hebrew *b'hemah*, which means 'beast'. As Fray Luis de León wrote in his *Exposición del Libro de Job*: 'Behemoth is a Hebrew word that stands for "beasts"; according to the received judgement of learned men, it means the elephant, so called because of its inordinate size; and being but a single animal it counts for many.'

We are also reminded of the fact that in the first verse of Genesis in the original text, the Hebrew name for God, *Elohím*, is plural, though the form of the verb it takes is singular – *Bereshit bará Elohím et hashamáim veet haáretz*. Trinitarians, by the way, have used this incongruity as an argument for the concept of the godhead being Three-in-One.

We give the ten verses in the translation from the Latin Vulgate by Father Knox (XL:10–19):

Here is Behemoth, my creature as thou art, fed on the same grass the oxen eat; yet what strength in his loins, what lustihood in the navel of his belly! Stiff as cedarwood his tail, close-knit the sinews of his groin, bones like pipes of bronze, gristle like plates of steel! None of God's works can vie with him, no weapon so strong in the hands of its maker; whole mountainsides, the playground of his

fellow beasts, he will lay under tribute, as he lies there
under the close covert of the marsh-reeds, thick boughs
for his shadow, among the willows by the stream. The
flooded river he drinks unconcerned; Jordan itself would
have no terrors for that gaping mouth. Like a lure it
would charm his eye, though it should pierce his nostrils
with sharp stakes.

The Brownies

Brownies are helpful little men of a brownish hue, which
gives them their name. It is their habit to visit Scottish farms
and, while the household sleeps, to perform domestic chores.
One of the tales by the Grimms deals with the same subject.

The famous writer Robert Louis Stevenson said he had
trained his Brownies in the craft of literature. Brownies
visited him in his dreams and told him wondrous tales; for
instance, the strange transformation of Dr Jekyll into the
diabolical Mr Hyde, and that episode of Olalla, in which the
scion of an old Spanish family bites his sister's hand.

Burak

In George Sale's translation (1734), the opening verse of
Chapter XVII of the Koran consists of these words: 'Praise be
unto him, who transported his servant by night, from the
sacred temple *of Mecca* to his farther temple of Jerusalem,

the circuit of which we have blessed, that we might show him *some* of our signs . . .' Commentators say that the one praised is God, that his servant is Mohammed, that the sacred temple is that of Mecca, that the distant temple is that of Jerusalem, and that from Jerusalem the Prophet was transported to the seventh heaven. In the oldest versions of the legend, Mohammed is guided by a man or an angel; in those of a later date he is furnished with a heavenly steed, larger than an ass and smaller than a mule. This steed is Burak, whose name means 'shining'. According to Richard Burton, translator of *The Book of a Thousand Nights and a Night*, Moslems in India usually picture Burak with a man's face, the ears of an ass, a horse's body, and the wings and tail of a peacock.

One of the Islamic legends tells that Burak, on leaving the ground, tipped a jar of water. The Prophet was taken up to the seventh heaven, along the way speaking in each of the heavens with the patriarchs and angels living there, and he crossed the Unity and felt a coldness that chilled his heart when the Lord laid a hand on his shoulder. Man's time is not commensurate with God's time; on his return the Prophet raised the jar, out of which not a single drop had yet been spilled.

Miguel Asín Palacios, the twentieth-century Spanish Orientalist, speaks of a mystic from Murcia of the 1200s who, in an allegory entitled the *Book of the Night Journey to the Majesty of the All-Generous*, has seen in Burak a symbol of divine love. In another text he speaks of the 'Burak of the pureness of heart'.

The Carbuncle

In mineralogy the carbuncle, from the Latin *carbunculus*, 'a little coal', is a ruby; as to the carbuncle of the ancients, it is supposed to have been a garnet.

In sixteenth-century South America, the name was given by the Spanish conquistadors to a mysterious animal – mysterious because nobody ever saw it well enough to know whether it was a bird or a mammal, whether it had feathers or fur. The poet-priest Martín del Barco Centenera, who claims to have seen it in Paraguay, describes it in his *Argentina* (1602) only as 'a smallish animal, with a shining mirror on its head, like a glowing coal . . .' Another conquistador, Gonzalo Fernández del Oviedo, associates this mirror or light shining out of the darkness – two of which he glimpsed in the Strait of Magellan – with the precious stone that dragons were thought to have hidden in their brain. He took his knowledge from Isidore of Seville, who wrote in his *Etymologies*:

> it is taken from the dragon's brain but does not harden into a gem unless the head is cut from the living beast; wizards, for this reason, cut the heads from sleeping dragons. Men bold enough to venture into dragon lairs scatter grain that has been doctored to make these beasts drowsy, and when they have fallen asleep their heads are struck off and the gems plucked out.

Here we are reminded of Shakespeare's toad (*As You Like It*, II, i), which, though 'ugly and venomous, Wears yet a precious jewel in his head . . .'

Possession of the Carbuncle's jewel offered fortune and luck. Barco Centenera underwent many hardships hunting the reaches of Paraguayan rivers and jungles for the elusive creature; he never found it. Down to this day we know nothing more about the beast and its secret head stone.

The Catoblepas

Pliny (VIII, 21) relates that somewhere on the borders of Ethiopia, near the head of the Nile, there is

> a wild beast called Catoblepes, little of body otherwise, heauy also and slow in al his limnes besides, but his head only is so great that his body is hardly able to beare it, he alwaies carrieth it downe to the earth, for if hee did not so, hee were able to kill all mankind; for there is not one that looketh vpon his eies, but he dies presently.

Catoblepas, in Greek, means 'that which looks downward'. The French naturalist Cuvier has conjectured that the gnu (contaminated by the basilisk and the gorgon) suggested the Catoblepas to the ancients. At the close of *The Temptation of Saint Anthony*, Flaubert describes it and has it speak in this way:

> black buffalo with the head of a hog, hanging close to the ground, joined to its body by a thin neck, long and loose as an emptied intestine.
> It wallows in the mud, and its legs are smothered under the huge mane of stiff bristles that hide its face.

> 'Obese, downhearted, wary, I do nothing but feel under my belly the warm mud. My head is so heavy that I cannot bear its weight. I wind it slowly around my body; with half-open jaws, I pull up with my tongue poisonous

35

plants dampened by my breath. Once, I ate up my fore-legs unawares.

'No one, Anthony, has ever seen my eyes; or else, those who have seen them have died. If I were to lift my eyelids – my pink and swollen eyelids – you would die on the spot.'

The Celestial Stag

We know absolutely nothing about the appearance of the Celestial Stag (maybe because nobody has ever had a good look at one), but we do know that these tragic animals live underground in mines and desire nothing more than to reach the light of day. They have the power of speech and implore the miners to help them to the surface. At first, a Celestial Stag attempts to bribe the workmen with the promise of revealing hidden veins of silver and gold; when this gambit fails, the beast becomes troublesome and the miners are forced to overpower it and wall it up in one of the mine galleries. It is also rumoured that miners outnumbered by the Stags have been tortured to death.

Legend has it that if the Celestial Stag finds its way into the open air, it becomes a foul-smelling liquid that can breed death and pestilence.

The tale is from China and is recorded by G. Willoughby-Meade in his book *Chinese Ghouls and Goblins*.

The Centaur

The Centaur is the most harmonious creature of fantastic zoology. 'Biform' it is called in Ovid's *Metamorphoses*, but its heterogeneous character is easily overlooked, and we tend to think that in the Platonic world of ideas there is an archetype of the Centaur as there is of the horse or the man. The discovery of this archetype took centuries; early archaic monuments show a naked man to whose waist the body and hind quarters of a horse are uncomfortably fixed. On the west façade of the Temple of Zeus at Olympia, the Centaurs already stand on the legs of a horse, and from the place where the animal's neck should start we find a human torso.

Centaurs were the offspring of Ixion, a king of Thessaly, and a cloud which Zeus had given the shape of Hera (or Juno); another version of the legend asserts that they were the offspring of Centaurus, Apollo's son, and Stilbia; a third, that they were the fruit of a union of Centaurus with the mares of Magnesium. (It is said that centaur is derived from *gandharva*; in Vedic myth, the *Gandharva*s are minor gods who drive the horses of the sun.) Since the art of riding was unknown to the Greeks of Homeric times, it has been conjectured that the first Scythian horseman they came across seemed to them all one with his horse, and it has also been alleged that the cavalry of the conquistadors were Centaurs to the Indians. A text quoted by Prescott runs as follows:

> One of the riders fell off his horse; and the Indians, seeing the animal fall asunder, up to now having deemed the beast all one, were so filled with terror that they turned and fled, crying out to their comrades that the animal had made itself into two and wondering at this: wherein we

may detect the secret hand of God; since, had this not happened, they might have slaughtered all the Christians.

But the Greeks, unlike the Indians, were familiar with the horse; it is more likely that the Centaur was a deliberate invention and not a confusion born of ignorance.

The best known of the Centaur fables is the one in which they battle with the Lapiths following a quarrel at a marriage celebration. To the Centaurs wine was now a new experience; in the midst of the banqueting an intoxicated Centaur insulted the bride and, overturning the tables, started the famous Centauromachy that Phidias, or a disciple of his, would carve on the Parthenon, that Ovid would commemorate in Book XII of the *Metamorphoses*, and that would inspire Rubens. Defeated by the Lapiths, the Centaurs were forced to leave Thessaly. Hercules, in a second encounter with them, all but annihilated the race of Centaurs with his arrows.

Anger and rustic barbarism are symbolized in the Centaur, but Chiron, 'the most righteous of the Centaurs' (*Iliad*, XI, 832), was the teacher of Achilles and Aesculapius, whom he instructed in the arts of music, hunting, and war, as well as medicine and surgery. Chiron stands out in Canto XII of the *Inferno*, generally known as the 'Canto of the Centaurs'. The acute observations of Momigliano in his 1945 edition of the *Commedia* should interest the curious.

Pliny (VII, 3) says he saw a Hippocentaur embalmed and preserved in honey that had been brought to Rome from Egypt in the reign of Claudius.

In the 'Feast of the Seven Sages', Plutarch humorously tells that one of the shepherds of Periander, a tyrant of Corinth, brought his master, in a leather pouch, a newborn creature that a mare had given birth to and whose face, neck, and arms were human while its body was that of a horse. It cried like a baby, and everyone thought it to be a frightening omen. The sage Thales examined it, chuckled, and said to Periander that really he could not approve his herdsmen's conduct.

In Book V of his poem *De rerum natura*, Lucretius declares the Centaur impossible since the equine species reaches maturity before the human, and at the age of three the Centaur would be a full-grown horse and a babbling child. The horse would die fifty years before the man.

Cerberus

If Hell is a house, the house of Hades, it is natural that it have its watchdog; it is also natural that this dog be fearful. Hesiod's *Theogony* gives it fifty heads; to make things easier for the plastic arts, this number has been reduced and Cerberus' three heads are now a matter of public record. Virgil speaks of its three throats; Ovid of its threefold bark; Butler compares the triple-crowned tiara of the Pope, who is Heaven's doorman, with the three heads of the dog who is the doorman of Hell (*Hudibras*, IV, 2). Dante lends it human characteristics which increase its infernal nature: a filthy black beard, clawed hands that in the lashing rain rip at the souls of the damned. It bites, barks, and bares its teeth.

Bringing Cerberus up into the light of day was the last of Hercules' tasks. ('He drow out Cerberus, the hound of helle,' writes Chaucer in 'The Monke's Tale'.) Zachary Grey, an English writer of the eighteenth century, in his commentary on *Hudibras* interprets the adventure in this way:

This Dog with three Heads denotes the past, the present, and the Time to come; which receive, and, as it were, devour all things. *Hercules* got the better of him, which shews that heroick Actions are always victorious over

Time, because they are present in the Memory of Posterity.

According to the oldest texts, Cerberus greets with his tail (which is a serpent) those entering into Hell, and tears to pieces those who try to get out. A later legend has him biting the newly arrived; to appease him a honeycake was placed in the coffin of the departed.

In Norse mythology, a blood-spattered dog, Garmr, keeps watch over the house of the dead and will fight against the gods when hell's wolves devour the moon and sun. Some give this dog four eyes; the dogs of Yama, the Brahman god of death, also have four eyes.

Both Brahmanism and Buddhism offer hells full of dogs, which, like Dante's Cerberus, are torturers of souls.

The Cheshire Cat
and the Kilkenny Cats

Everyone is familiar with the phrase 'grin like a Cheshire cat', which means of course to put on a sardonic face. Many explanations of its origin have been attempted. One is that in Cheshire cheeses were sold in the shape of the grinning head of a cat. Another, that Cheshire is a Palatine country or earldom and that this mark of nobility provoked the hilarity of its cats. Still another is that in the time of Richard III there was a gamewarden named Caterling who used to break into an angry smile whenever he crossed swords with poachers.

In *Alice in Wonderland*, published in 1865, Lewis Carroll endowed the Cheshire Cat with the faculty of slowly disappearing to the point of leaving only its grin – without teeth and without a mouth. Of the Kilkenny Cats it is told that they got into raging quarrels and devoured each other, leaving behind no more than their tails. This story goes back to the eighteenth century.

The Chimera

The first mention we have of the Chimera is in Book VI of the *Iliad*. There Homer writes that it came of divine stock and was a lion in its foreparts, a goat in the middle, and a serpent in its hindparts, and that from its mouth it vomited flames, and finally was killed by the handsome Bellerophon, the son of Glaucus, following the signs of the gods. A lion's head, goat's belly, and serpent's tail is the most obvious image conveyed by Homer's words, but Hesiod's *Theogony* describes the Chimera as having three heads, and this is the way it is depicted in the famous Arezzo bronze that dates from the fifth century. Springing from the middle of the animal's back is the head of a goat, while at one end it has a snake's head and at the other a lion's.

The Chimera reappears in the sixth book of the *Aeneid*, 'armed with flame'; Virgil's commentator Servius Honoratus observed that, according to all authorities, the monster was native to Lycia, where there was a volcano bearing its name. The base of this mountain was infested with serpents, higher up on its flanks were meadows and goats, and towards its desolate top, which belched out flames, a pride of lions had its resort. The Chimera would seem to be a metaphor of this strange elevation. Earlier, Plutarch suggested that Chimera was the name of a pirate captain who adorned his ships with the images of a lion, a goat, and a snake.

These absurd hypotheses are proof that the Chimera was beginning to bore people. Easier than imagining it was to translate it into something else. As a beast it was too heterogeneous; the lion, goat, and snake (in some texts, dragon) do not readily make up a single animal. With time the Chimera tended to become 'chimerical'; a celebrated joke of Rabelais ('Can a chimera, swinging in the void, swallow second intentions?') clearly marks the transition. The patchwork image disappeared but the word remained, signifying the impossible. A vain or foolish fancy is the definition of Chimera that we now find in dictionaries.

The Chinese Dragon

Chinese cosmogony teaches that the Ten Thousand Beings or Archetypes (the world) are born of the rhythmic conjunction of the two complementary eternal principles, the *yin* and the *yang*. Corresponding to the *yin* are concentration, darkness, passivity, even numbers, and cold; to the *yang*, growth, light, activity, odd numbers, and heat. Symbols of the *yin* are women, the earth, the colour orange, valleys, riverbeds, and the tiger; of the *yang*, men, the sky, blue, mountains, pillars, the dragon.

The Chinese Dragon, the *lung*, is one of the four magic animals. (The others are the unicorn, the phoenix, and the tortoise.) At best, the Western Dragon spreads terror; at worst, it is a figure of fun. The *lung* of Chinese myth, however, is divine and is like an angel that is also a lion. We read in the *Historical Record* of Ssu-ma Ch'ien that Confucius went to consult the archivist or librarian Lao-tzu, and after his visit said:

Birds fly, fish swim, animals run. The running animal

can be caught in a trap, the swimmer in a net, and the flyer by an arrow. But there is the Dragon; I don't know how it rides on the wind or how it reaches the heavens. Today I met Lao-tzu and I can say that I have seen the Dragon.

It was a Dragon, or a Dragon Horse, which emerged from the Yellow River to reveal to an emperor the famous circular diagram symbolizing the reciprocal play of the *yang* and *yin*. A certain king had in his stables saddle Dragons and draft Dragons; one emperor fed on Dragons, and his kingdom prospered. A famous poet, to illustrate the risks of greatness, wrote: 'The unicorn ends up coldcuts; the dragon as meat pie.'

In the *I Ching* or *Book of Changes*, the Dragon signifies wisdom. For centuries it was the imperial emblem. The emperor's throne was called the Dragon Throne, his face the Dragon Face. On announcing an emperor's death, it was said that he had ascended to heaven on the back of a Dragon.

Popular imagination links the Dragon to clouds, to the rainfall needed by farmers, and to great rivers. 'The earth couples with the dragon' is a common phrase for rain. About the sixth century, Chang Seng-yu executed a wall painting that depicted four Dragons. Viewers complained that he had left out their eyes. Annoyed, Chang picked up his brushes again and completed two of the twisted figures. Then 'the air was filled with thunder and lightning, the wall cracked and the Dragons ascended to heaven. But the other two eyeless Dragons remained in place'.

The Chinese Dragon has horns, claws, and scales, and its backbone prickles with spines. It is commonly pictured with a pearl, which it swallows or spits up. In this pearl lies its power; the Dragon is tamed if the pearl is taken from it.

Chuang Tzu tells us of a determined man who at the end of three thankless years mastered the art of slaying Dragons, and for the rest of his days was not given a single chance to put his art into practice.

43

The Chinese Fox

In everyday zoology the Chinese Fox differs little from other Foxes, but not so in fantastic zoology. Statistics give it a life-span that varies between eight hundred and a thousand years. The animal is considered a bad omen, and each part of its anatomy enjoys some special power. It has only to strike the ground with its tail to start a fire; it can see into the future; and it can change into many forms, preferably into old men, young ladies, and scholars. It is astute, wary, and sceptical; its pleasures lie in playing pranks and in causing torment. Men, when they die, may transmigrate with the body of a Fox. Its dwelling is close by graves. There are thousands of stories and legends concerning it; we transcribe one, a tale by the ninth-century poet Niu Chiao, which is not without its humorous side:

Wang saw two Foxes standing on their hind legs and lean-ing against a tree. One of them held a sheet of paper in its hand, and they laughed together as though they were shar-ing a joke. Wang tried to frighten them off but they stood their ground, and finally he shot at the one holding the page. The Fox was hit in the eye and Wang took away the piece of paper. At the inn Wang told the story to the other guests. While he spoke a gentleman having a bandaged eye came in. He listened to Wang's story with interest and asked if he might not be shown the paper. Wang was just about to pro-duce it when the innkeeper noticed that the newcomer had a tail. 'He's a Fox!' he shouted, and on the spot the gentleman turned into a Fox and fled. The Foxes tried time after time to recover the paper, which was filled with indecipherable writing, but were repeatedly set back. Wang decided at last to return home. On the road he met his whole family, who were on their way to the capital. They said that he had ordered them to undertake the journey, and his mother showed him the letter in which he asked them to sell off all their property and join him in the city. Wang, studying the letter, saw that the page was blank. Although they no longer had a roof over their heads, he ordered, 'Let's go back.'

One day a younger brother appeared whom everyone had given up for dead. He asked about the family's misfortunes and Wang told him the whole story. 'Ah,' said the brother when Wang came to the part about the Foxes, 'there lies the root of all the evil.' Wang showed him the page in question. Tearing it from Wang's hand, the brother stuffed the sheet into his pocket and said, 'At last I have back what I wanted.' Then, changing himself into a Fox, he made his escape.

The Chinese Phoenix

The sacred books of the Chinese may be disappointing for the reason that they lack the pathetic element to which we have been accustomed by the Bible. But occasionally, all at once in their even-tempered discourse, we are moved by some intimacy. This one, for instance, recorded in Book VII of the Confucian *Analects* (Waley translation):

> The Master said, How utterly have things gone to the bad with me! It is long now indeed since I dreamed that I saw the Duke of Chou.

Or this one from Book IX:

> The Master said, The phoenix does not come; the river gives forth no chart. It is all over with me!

The chart, or sign (explain the commentaries), refers to an inscription on the back of a magical tortoise. As for the

Phoenix, it is a bird of brilliant colours, not unlike the pheasant and peacock. In prehistoric times it visited the gardens and palaces of virtuous emperors as a visible token of celestial favour. The male (Feng), which had three legs, lived in the sun. The female is the Huang; together they are the emblem of everlasting love.

In the first century A.D., the daring unbeliever Wang Ch'ung denied that the Phoenix constituted a determined species. He said that just as the serpent turns into a fish and the rat into a tortoise, the stag in times of widespread prosperity takes the form of the unicorn, and the goose that of the Phoenix. He explained these mutations by the 'well-known liquid' which, some 2,356 years B.C., in the courtyard of Yao – who was one of the model emperors – had made the grass grow scarlet. As may be seen, his information was deficient, or rather, excessive.

In the Infernal Regions there is an imaginary structure known as the Tower of the Phoenix.

Chronos or Hercules

The treatise *Difficulties and Solutions of First Principles* by the Neoplatonist Damascus (born about A.D. 480) records a strange version of the theogony and cosmogony of Orphism, in which Chronos – or Hercules – is a monster:

> According to Hieronymus and Hellanicus (if the two are not one), Orphic doctrine teaches that in the beginning there was water and mud, with which the earth was shaped. These two principles were taught to be the first: water and earth. From them came the third, a winged dragon, which in its foreparts had the head of a bull, in its hindparts the head of a lion, and in its middle the face of a

god; this dragon was named the *Unageing Chronos* and also *Heracles*. With him Necessity, also known as the Inevitable, was born and spread to the boundaries of the Universe ... Chronos, the dragon, drew from himself a threefold seed: moist Ether, limitless Chaos, and misty Erebus. Under them he laid an egg, from which the world was to hatch. The last principle was a god who was man and woman, with golden wings on its back, and bulls' heads on its sides, and on its head a huge dragon, like all manner of beasts ...

Perhaps because what is excessively monstrous seems less fitting to Greece than to the East, Walter Kranz attributes an Oriental origin to these fancies.

A Creature Imagined
by C. S. Lewis

Slowly, shakily, with unnatural and inhuman movements a human form, scarlet in the firelight, crawled out on to the floor of the cave. It was the Un-man, of course: dragging its broken leg and with its lower jaw sagging open like that of a corpse, it raised itself to a standing position. And then, close behind it, something else came up out of the hole. First came what looked like branches of trees, and then seven or eight spots of light, irregularly grouped like a constellation. Then a tubular mass which reflected the red glow as if it were polished. His heart gave a great leap as the branches suddenly resolved themselves into long wiry feelers and the dotted lights became the many eyes of a shell-helmeted head and the mass that followed it was revealed as a large roughly cylindrical body.

47

Horrible things followed – angular, many jointed legs, and presently, when he thought the whole body was in sight, a second body came following it and after that a third. The thing was in three parts, united only by a kind of wasp's waist structure – three parts that did not seem to be truly aligned and made it look as if it had been trodden on – a huge, many legged, quivering deformity, standing just behind the Un-man so that the horrible shadows of both danced in enormous and united menace on the wall of rock behind them.

C. S. LEWIS: *Perelandra*

The Crocotta and the Leucrocotta

Ctesias, physician to Artaxerxes Mnemon in the fourth century B.C., made use of Persian sources to compile a description of India, a work of incalculable value if we are curious as to how Persians under Artaxerxes Mnemon imagined India. In Chapter 32, he gives an account of the cynolycus, or dog-wolf, from which Pliny seems to have evolved his Crocotta. Pliny writes (VIII, 21) that the Crocotta is an animal 'ingendred betwixt a dog and a Wolfe: these are able to crash with their teeth all they can come by: and a thing is no sooner downe their swallow, and got into their stomacke, but presently they digest it'. He goes on to describe another Indian animal, the Leucrocotta, as follows:

a most swift beast, as big almost as an he Asse, legged like an Hart, with a necke, taile, and brest of a Lion, headed like these grayes or Badgers, with a clouen foot in twaine:

the slit of his mouth reacheth to his eares, in stead of teeth an entire whole bone. They report that this beast feigneth a mans voice.

Later authorities seem to feel that Pliny's Leucrocotta is a cumbersome blend of the Indian antelope and the hyena. All of these animals Pliny has fit into an Ethiopian landscape, where he also lodges a wild bull with convenient movable horns, a hide as hard as flint, and hair turned contrariwise.

A Crossbreed

I have a curious animal, half-cat, half-lamb. It is a legacy from my father. But it only developed in my time; formerly it was far more lamb than cat. Now it is both in about equal parts. From the cat it takes its head and claws, from the lamb its size and shape; from both its eyes, which are wild and changing, its hair, which is soft, lying close to its body, its movements, which partake both of skipping and slinking. Lying on the window-sill in the sun it curls itself up in a ball and purrs; out in the meadow it rushes about as if mad and is scarcely to be caught. It flies from cats and makes to attack lambs. On moonlight nights its favourite promenade is the tiles. It cannot mew and it loathes rats. Beside the hen-coop it can lie for hours in ambush, but it has never yet seized an opportunity for murder.

I feed it on milk; that seems to suit it best. In long draughts it sucks the milk into it through its teeth of a beast of prey. Naturally it is a great source of entertainment for children. Sunday morning is the visiting hour. I sit with the little beast on my knees, and the children of the whole neighbourhood stand round me.

Then the strangest questions are asked, which no

human being could answer: Why there is only one such animal, why I rather than anybody else should own it, whether there was ever an animal like it before and what would happen if it died, whether it feels lonely, why it has no children, what it is called, etc.

I never trouble to answer, but confine myself without further explanation to exhibiting my possession. Sometimes the children bring cats with them; once they actually brought two lambs. But against all their hopes there was no scene of recognition. The animals gazed calmly at each other with their animal eyes, and obviously accepted their reciprocal existence as a divine fact.

Sitting on my knees the beast knows neither fear nor lust of pursuit. Pressed against me it is happiest. It remains faithful to the family that brought it up. In that there is certainly no extraordinary mark of fidelity, but merely the true instinct of an animal which, though it has countless step-relations in the world, has perhaps not a single blood relation, and to which consequently the protection it has found with us is sacred.

Sometimes I cannot help laughing when it sniffs round me and winds itself between my legs and simply will not be parted from me. Not content with being lamb and cat, it almost insists on being a dog as well. Once when, as may happen to any one, I could see no way out of my business difficulties and all that depends on such things, and had resolved to let everything go, and in this mood was lying in my rocking-chair in my room, the beast on my knees, I happened to glance down and saw tears dropping from its huge whiskers. Were they mine, or were they the animal's? Had this cat, along with the soul of a lamb, the ambitions of a human being? I did not inherit much from my father, but this legacy is worth looking at.

It has the restlessness of both beasts, that of the cat and that of the lamb, diverse as they are. For that reason its skin feels too narrow for it. Sometimes it jumps up on the armchair beside me, plants its front legs on my shoulder, and puts its muzzle to my ear. It is as if it were saying something to me, and as a matter of fact it turns its head afterwards and gazes in my face to see the impression its communication has made. And to oblige it I behave as if I had understood and nod. Then it jumps to the floor and dances about with joy.

Perhaps the knife of the butcher would be a release for this animal; but as it is a legacy I must deny it that. So it must wait until the breath voluntarily leaves its body, even though it sometimes gazes at me with a look of human understanding, challenging me to do the thing of which both of us are thinking.

FRANZ KAFKA: *Description of a Struggle*

(Translated from the German by
Tania and James Stern)

The Double

Suggested or stimulated by reflections in mirrors and in water and by twins, the idea of the Double is common to many countries. It is likely that sentences such as *A friend is another self* by Pythagoras or the Platonic *Know thyself* were inspired by it. In Germany this Double is called *Doppelgänger*, which means 'double walker'. In Scotland there is the *fetch*, which comes to fetch a man to bring him to his death; there is also the Scottish word *wraith* for an apparition thought to be seen by a person in his exact image just before death. To meet oneself is, therefore, ominous. The tragic ballad 'Ticonderoga' by Robert Louis Stevenson tells of a legend on this theme. There is also the strange picture by Rossetti ('How They Met Themselves') in which two lovers come upon themselves in the dusky gloom of a wood. We may also cite examples from Hawthorne ('Howe's Masquerade'), Dostoyevsky, Alfred de Musset, James ('The Jolly Corner'), Kleist, Chesterton ('The Mirror of Madmen'), and Hearn (*Some Chinese Ghosts*).

The ancient Egyptians believed that the Double, the *ka*, was a man's exact counterpart, having his same walk and his same dress. Not only men, but gods and beasts, stones and trees, chairs and knives had their *ka*, which was invisible except to certain priests who could see the Doubles of the gods and were granted by them a knowledge of things past and things to come.

To the Jews the appearance of one's Double was not an omen of imminent death. On the contrary, it was proof of having attained prophetic powers. This is how it is explained by Gershom Scholem. A legend recorded in the Talmud tells the story of a man who, in search of God, met himself.

In the story 'William Wilson' by Poe, the Double is the hero's conscience. He kills it and dies. In a similar way, Dorian Gray in Wilde's novel stabs his portrait and meets his death. In Yeats's poems the Double is our other side, our opposite, the one who complements us, the one we are not nor will ever become.

Plutarch writes that the Greeks gave the name *other self* to a king's ambassador.

The Eastern Dragon

The Dragon has the ability to assume many shapes, but these are inscrutable. Generally, it is imagined with a head something like a horse's, with a snake's tail, with wings on its sides (if at all), and with four claws, each furnished with four curved nails. We read also of its nine resemblances: its horns are not unlike those of a stag, its head that of a camel, its eyes those of a devil, its neck that of a snake, its belly that of a clam, its scales those of a fish, its talons those of an eagle, its footprints those of a tiger, and its ears those of an ox. There are specimens of the Dragon that lack ears and hear with their horns. It is customary to picture them with a pearl, which dangles from their necks and is a symbol of the sun. Within this pearl lies the Dragon's power. The beast is rendered helpless if its pearl is stolen from it.

History traces the earliest emperors back to Dragons. Their teeth, bones, and saliva all possess medicinal qualities. According to its will, the Dragon can become visible or invisible. In springtime it ascends into the skies; in the fall it dives down into the depths of the seas. Some Dragons lack wings yet fly under their own impetus. Science distinguishes several kinds. The Celestial Dragon carries on its back the palaces of the gods that otherwise might fall to earth, destroying the cities of men; the Divine Dragon makes the winds and rains for the benefit of mankind; the Terrestrial Dragon determines the course of streams and rivers; the Subterranean Dragon stands watch over treasures forbidden to men. The Buddhists affirm that Dragons are no fewer in number than the fishes of their many concentric seas; somewhere in the universe a sacred cipher exists to express their exact number. The Chinese believe in Dragons more than in any other deities because Dragons are frequently seen in the changing formations of clouds. Similarly, Shakespeare has observed, 'Sometime we see a cloud that's dragonish.'

The Dragon rules over mountains, is linked to geomancy, dwells near tombs, is connected with the cult of Confucius, is the Neptune of the seas, and appears also on terra firma.

The Sea-Dragon Kings live in resplendent underwater palaces and feed on opals and pearls. Of these Kings there are five: the chief is in the middle, the other four correspond to the cardinal points. Each stretches some three or four miles in length; on changing position, they cause mountains to tumble. They are sheathed in an armour of yellow scales, and their muzzles are whiskered. Their legs and tail are shaggy, their forehead juts over their flaming eyes, their ears are small and thick, their mouths gape open, their tongues are long, and teeth sharp. Their breath boils up and roasts whole shoals of fishes. When these Sea Dragons rise to the ocean surface, they cause whirlpools and typhoons; when they take to the air they blow up storms that rip the roofs off the houses of entire cities and flood the countryside. The Dragon Kings are immortal and can communicate among themselves, without recourse to words, in spite of any distance that separates them. It is during the third month that they make their annual report to the upper heavens.

The Eater of the Dead

There is a strange literary genre which, spontaneously, has sprung up in various lands and at various times. This is the manual for the guidance of the dead through the Other World. *Heaven and Hell* by Swedenborg, the writings of the Gnostics, the Tibetan *Bardo Thödol* (which, according to Evans-Wentz, should be translated as 'Liberation by Hearing on the After-Death Plane'), and the Egyptian *Book of the Dead* do not exhaust the possible examples. The similarities and differences of the latter two books have attracted the attention of esoteric scholarship; for us, let it be enough to recall that in the Tibetan manual the Other World is as illusory as this one, while to the Egyptians it has a real and objective existence.

In both texts there is a Judgement Scene before a jury of deities, some with the heads of apes; in both, a symbolical weighing of evil and good deeds. In the *Book of the Dead*, a heart and a feather are weighed against each other, 'the heart representing the conduct or conscience of the deceased and the feather righteousness or truth'. In the *Bardo Thödol*, white pebbles and black pebbles are placed on either side of the balance. The Tibetans have demons or devils who lead the condemned to the place of purgation in a hell-world; the Egyptians have a grim monster attending their wicked, an Eater of the Dead.

The dead man swears not to have caused hunger or sorrow, not to have killed or to have made others kill for him, not to have stolen the food set aside for the dead, not to have used false weights, not to have taken the milk from a baby's mouth, not to have driven livestock from their pasturage, not to have netted the birds of the gods.

If he lies, the forty-two judges deliver him to the Eater, 'who has the head of a crocodile, the trunk of a lion, and the hinder parts of a hippopotamus'. The Eater is assisted by another animal Babaí, of whom we know only that he is frightening and that Plutarch identifies him with the Titan who fathered the Chimera.

The Eight-Forked Serpent

The Eight-Forked Serpent of Koshi is prominent in the mythical cosmogony of Japan. It was eight-headed and eight-tailed; its eyes were red as the winter cherry, and pine trees and mosses grew on its back, while firs sprouted on each of its heads. As it crawled, it stretched over eight valleys and eight hills, and its belly was always flecked with blood. In seven years this beast had devoured seven maidens, the daughters of a king, and in the eighth year was about to eat up the youngest daughter, named Princess-Comb-Ricefield. The Princess was saved by a god who bore the name of Brave-Swift-Impetuous-Male. This knight built a circular enclosure of wood with eight gates and eight platforms at each gate. On the platforms he set tubs of rice beer. The Eight-Forked Serpent came and, dipping a head into each of the tubs, gulped down the beer and was soon fast asleep. Then Brave-Swift-Impetuous-Male lopped the heads. A river of blood sprang from the necks. In the Serpent's tail a sword was found that to this day commands veneration in the Great Shrine of Atsuta. These events took place on the mountain formerly named Serpent-Mountain and now called Eight-Cloud Mountain. The number eight in Japan is a magic number and stands for *many*, just as forty ('When forty winters shall besiege thy brow') did in Elizabethan England. Japanese paper currency still commemorates the killing of the Serpent.

It is superfluous to point out that the redeemer married the redeemed, as in Hellenic myth Perseus married Andromeda.

In his English rendering of the cosmogonies and theogonies of old Japan (*The Sacred Scriptures of the Japanese*), Post Wheeler also records analogous legends of the Hydra of Greek myth, of Fafnir from the Germanic, and of the Egyptian goddess Hathor, whom a god made drunk with blood-red beer so that mankind would be saved from annihilation.

The Elephant That Foretold
the Birth of the Buddha

Five centuries before the Christian era, Queen Maya, in Nepal, had a dream that a white Elephant, which dwelled on the Golden Mountain, had entered her body. This visionary beast was furnished with six tusks. The King's soothsayers predicted that the Queen would bear a son who would become either ruler of the world or the saviour of mankind. As is common knowledge, the latter came true.

In India the Elephant is a domestic animal. White stands for humility and the number six is sacred, corresponding to the six dimensions of space: upward, downward, forward, back, left, and right.

The Eloi and the Morlocks

The hero of the novel *The Time Machine*, which a young writer Herbert George Wells published in 1895, travels on a mechanical device into an unfathomable future. There he finds that mankind has split into two species: the Eloi, who are frail and defenceless aristocrats living in idle gardens and feeding on the fruits of the trees; and the Morlocks, a race of underground proletarians who, after ages of labouring in darkness, have gone blind, but driven by the force of the past, go on working at their rusted intricate machinery that produces nothing. Shafts with winding staircases unite the two worlds. On moonless nights, the Morlocks climb up out of their caverns and feed on the Eloi.

The nameless hero, pursued by Morlocks, escapes back into the present. He brings with him as a solitary token of his adventure an unknown flower that falls into dust and that will not blossom on earth until thousands and thousands of years are over.

The Elves

The Elves are of Nordic origin. Little is known about what they look like, except that they are tiny and sinister. They steal cattle and children and also take pleasure in minor acts of deviltry. In England, the word 'elflock' was given to a tangle of hair because it was supposed to be a trick of the Elves. An Anglo-Saxon charm, which for all we know may go back to heathen times, credits them with the mischievous habit of shooting, from afar, miniature arrows of iron that break the surface of the skin without a trace and are at the root of sudden painful stitches. In the Younger Edda, a distinction is noted between Light Elves and Dark: 'The Light Elves are fairer than a glance of the sun, the Dark Elves blacker than pitch.' The German for nightmare is *Alp*; etymology traces the word back to 'elf', since it was commonly believed in the Middle Ages that Elves weighed heavily upon the breast of sleepers, giving them bad dreams.

An Experimental Account of What Was Known, Seen, and Met by Mrs Jane Lead in London in 1694

Among the many writings of the blind English mystic Jane Lead (or Leade) is to be found *The Wonders of God's Creation manifested in the variety of Eight Worlds, as they were known experimentally unto the Author* (London, 1695). About this time, as Mrs Lead's fame spread throughout Holland and Germany, her work was done into Dutch by an eager young scholar, H. van Ameyden van Duym. But later on when, due to the jealousies of her disciples, the authenticity of certain manuscripts was disputed, it became necessary for the van Duym versions to be retranslated into English. On page 340 (10 B) of the *Eight Worlds*, we read:

Salamanders have their appointed Dwelling in Fire; Sylphs in the Air; Nymphs in the flowing Waters; and Gnomes in Earthen-burrows, but the creature whose substance is Bliss is everywhere at home. All sounds, even to the roaring of Lions, the screeching of the nightly Owls, the laments and groans of those entrapped in Hell, are as sweet Musick to her. All odours, even to the foulest stench of Corruption, are to her as the delight of roses and Lilies. All savours, even to the banquet-table of the Harpys of heathen lore, are as Sweet loaves and spiced Ale. Wandering at noon through the Waste-Places of the world, it seems to her she is refreshed by Canopies of flocking Angels. The earnest seeker will look for her in All places, however dim and sordid, of this world or in the seven others. Thrust a keen Sword-blade through her and it will seem as a fountain of Divine and Pure pleasure. These eyes, by Translation, have been given to see her ways; and an equal gift as revealed by Wisdom is sometimes granted the Child.

The Fairies

They meddle magically in human affairs, and their name is linked to the Latin word *fatum* (fate, destiny). It is said that the Fairies are the most numerous, the most beautiful, and the most memorable of the minor supernatural beings. They are not restricted to a particular place or particular period. Ancient Greeks, Eskimos, and Red Indians all tell stories of heroes who have won the love of these creatures of the imagination. Such fortunes hold their perils; a Fairy, once its whim is satisfied, may deal death to its lovers.

In Ireland and Scotland 'the people of Faery' are assigned underground dwelling places, where they confine children and men whom they have kidnapped. Believing that the flint arrowheads they dig up in the fields once belonged to Fairies. Irish farmers endow these objects with unfailing medical powers. Yeats's early tales abound in accounts of village people among the Fairies. In one a countrywoman tells him that

> she did not believe either in Hell or in ghosts. Hell was an invention got up by the priest to keep people good; and the ghosts would not be permitted, she held, to go 'trapsin' about the earth' at their own free will; 'but there are faeries and little leprechauns, and water-horses, and fallen angels'.

Fairies are fond of song and music and the colour green.

Yeats notes that 'The [little] people and faeries in Ireland are sometimes as big as we are, sometimes bigger, and sometimes, as I have been told, about three feet high.' At the end of the seventeenth century a Scots churchman, the Reverend Robert Kirk of Aberfoyle, wrote a work entitled *The Secret Commonwealth; or an Essay on the Nature and Actions of the Subterranean (and for the most part) Invisible People heretofoir going under the name of Faunes and Fairies, or the lyke, among the Low Country Scots, as they are described by those who have the second sight*. In 1815, Sir Walter Scott had the book reprinted. Of Mr Kirk it is told that the Fairies snatched him away because he had revealed their mysteries.

On the seas off Italy, especially in the Strait of Messina, the fata morgana contrives mirages to confuse sailors and lure them aground.

Fastitocalon

The Middle Ages attributed to the Holy Ghost the composition of two books. The first was, as is well known, the Bible; the second, the whole world, whose creatures had locked up in them moral teachings. In order to explain these teachings, Physiologi, or Bestiaries, were compiled in which accounts of birds and beasts and fishes were laid over with allegorical applications. Out of an Anglo-Saxon bestiary, we take the following text, translated by R. K. Gordon:

Now by my wit I will also speak in a poem, a song, about a kind of fish, about the mighty whale. He to our sorrow is often found dangerous and fierce to all seafaring men. The name Fastitocalon is given him, the floater on ocean streams. His form is like a roughstone, as if the greatest of seaweeds, girt by sand-banks, were heaving by the water's shore, so that seafarers suppose they behold some island with their eyes; and then they fasten the high-prowed ships with cables to the false land, tie the sea steeds at the water's edge, and then undaunted go up into that island. The ships remain fast by the shore, encompassed by water. Then, wearied out, the sailors encamp, look not for danger. On the island they kindle fire, build a great blaze; the men, worn out, are in gladness, longing for rest. When he, skilled in treachery, feels that the voyagers are set firmly upon him, are encamped, rejoicing in the clear weather, then suddenly the ocean creature sinks down with his prey into the salt wave, seeks the depths, and then delivers the ships and the men to drown in the hall of death.

He, the proud voyager, has another habit, yet more wondrous. When on the ocean hunger harries him ... then the warden of the ocean opens his mouth, his lips wide. A pleasant smell comes from within, so that other kinds of fish are betrayed thereby; they swim swiftly to where the sweet smell issues forth. They enter there in a thoughtless throng, till the wide jaw is filled. Then suddenly the fierce jaws snap together, enclosing the plunder. Thus is it for every man who ... lets himself be snared by a sweet smell, a false desire, so that he is guilty of sins against the King of glory.

This same story is told in the *Arabian Nights*, in St Brendan's legend, and in Milton's *Paradise Lost*, which shows us the whale 'slumbering on the Norway foam'. Professor Gordon tells us that 'In earlier versions the creature was a turtle and was named Aspidochelone. In course of time the name became corrupted, and the whale replaced the turtle.'

Fauna of Chile

Our chief authority on animals incubated by the Chilean imagination is Julio Vicuña Cifuentes, whose *Myths and Superstitions* collects a number of legends drawn from oral tradition. All of the following extracts but one are taken from this work. *The Calchona* is recorded in Zorobabel Rodríguez' *Dictionary of Chileanisms*, published in Santiago de Chile in 1875.

The *Alicanto* is a nocturnal bird that seeks its food in veins of gold and silver. The variety that feeds on gold may be identified by the golden light that gleams from its wings when it runs with them open (for it cannot fly); the silver-feeding Alicanto is known, as one might expect, by a silvery light.

The fact that the bird is flightless is not due to its wings, which are perfectly normal, but to the heavy metallic meals that weigh down its crop. When hungry it runs swiftly; when gorged it is hardly able to crawl.

Prospectors or mining engineers believe their fortune is made if they are lucky enough to have an Alicanto for a guide, since the bird may lead them to the discovery of hidden ore. Nevertheless, the prospector should be very careful, for, if the bird suspects it is being followed, it dims its light and slips away in the dark. It may also suddenly change its path and draw its pursuer towards a chasm.

The *Calchona* is a kind of Newfoundland dog woollier than an unshorn ram and more bearded than a billy goat. White in colour, it chooses dark nights to appear before mountain travellers, snatching their lunch baskets from them and muttering sullen threats; it also scares horses, hunts down outlaws, and works all sorts of evil.

The *Chonchón* has the shape of a human head; its ears, which are extremely large, serve as wings for its flight on moonless nights. Chonchónes are supposed to be endowed with all the powers of wizards. They are dangerous when molested, and many fables are told about them.

There are several ways to bring these flying creatures down when they pass overhead intoning their ominous *tué*, *tué tué*, the only sign that betrays their presence, since they are invisible to anyone not a wizard. The following are judiciously advised: to recite or sing a prayer known only to a few who stubbornly refuse to divulge it; to chant a certain twelve words twice over; to mark a Solomon's seal on the ground; and lastly, to spread open a waistcoat and lay it out in a specified way. The Chonchón falls, flapping its wings furiously, and cannot lift itself again no matter how hard it tries until another Chonchón comes to its aid. Generally, the incident does not conclude here, for sooner or later the Chonchón wreaks its vengeance on whomever has mocked at it.

Creditable witnesses have told the following story. In a house in Limache where visitors had gathered one night, the disorderly cries of a Chonchón were suddenly heard outside. Someone made the sign of Solomon's seal, and a heavy object fell into the backyard; it was a large bird the size of a turkey and had a head with red wattles. They cut the head off, gave it to a dog, and threw the body up on the roof. At once they heard a deafening uproar of Chonchónes, at the same time noting that the dog's belly had swollen as though the animal had gulped down the head of a person. The next morning they searched in vain for the Chonchón's body; it had disappeared from the roof. Somewhat later the town gravedigger reported that on that same day several unknown persons had come to bury a body which, when they had gone away, he found to be headless.

The *Hide* is an octopus that lives in the sea and has the dimensions and appearance of a cowhide stretched out flat. Its edges are furnished with numberless eyes, and, in that part which seems to be its head, it has four more eyes of a larger size. Whenever persons or animals enter the water, the Hide rises to the surface and engulfs them with an irresistible force, devouring them in a matter of moments.

The *Huallepén* is an amphibious animal that is fierce, powerful, and shy; under three feet tall, it has a calf's head and a sheep's body. On the spur of the moment it mounts sheep and cows, fathering in them offspring of the same species as the mother but which can be spotted by their twisted hooves and sometimes by their twisted muzzles. A pregnant woman who sees a Huallepén, or hears its bellow, or who dreams of it three nights in a row, gives birth to a deformed child. The same happens if she sees an animal begotten by the Huallepén.

The *Strong Toad* is an imaginary animal different from other toads in that its back is covered with a shell like that of a turtle. This Toad glows in the dark like a firefly and is so tough that the only way to kill it is to reduce it to ashes. It owes its name to the great power of its stare, which it uses to attract or repel whatever is in its range.

Fauna of China

The following list of strange animals is taken from the *T'ai P'ing Kuang Chi* (Extensive Records Made in the Period of Peace and Prosperity), completed in the year 978 and published in 981:

The *Celestial Horse* is like a white dog with a black head. It has fleshy wings and can fly.

The *Chiang-liang* has a tiger's head, a man's face, long limbs, four hooves, and a snake between its teeth.

In the region to the west of the Red Water dwells the beast known as the *Ch'ou-t'i*, which has a head both front and back.

The denizens of Ch'uan-T'ou have human heads, the wings of a bat, and a bird's beak. They feed exclusively on raw fish.

In the Country of Long Arms, the hands of the inhabitants dangle to the ground. They live by catching fish at the edge of the sea.

The *Hsiao* is similar to the owl but has a man's face, an ape's body, and a dog's tail. Its presence foretells prolonged drought.

The *Hsing-hsing* are like apes. They have white faces and pointed ears. They walk upright, like men, and climb trees.

The *Hsing-t'ien* is a being that was decapitated for having fought against the gods, and so it has remained forever headless. Its eyes are in its chest and its navel is its mouth. It hops up and down and jumps about in clearings and other open places, and brandishes a shield and axe.

The *Hua-fish*, or flying snakefish, appears to be a fish but has the wings of a bird. Its appearance forebodes a period of drought.

The mountain *Hui* looks like a dog with a human head. It is a fine jumper and moves with the swiftness of an arrow; this is why its appearance is held to foretell the coming of typhoons. On beholding a man, the Hui laughs mockingly.

The *Musical Serpent* has a serpent's head and four wings. It makes sounds like those of the Musical Stone.

The *Ocean Men* have human heads and arms, and the body and tail of a fish. They come to the surface in stormy weather.

The *Ping-feng*, which lives in the country of Magical Water, resembles a black pig with a head at each end.

In the region of the Queer Arm, people have a single arm and three eyes. They are exceptionally skilful and build flying chariots in which they travel on the winds.

The *Ti-chiang* is a supernatural bird dwelling in the Mountains of the Sky. Its colour is bright red, it has six feet and four wings, but has neither face nor eyes.

Fauna of Mirrors

In one of the volumes of the *Lettres édifiantes et curieuses* that appeared in Paris during the first half of the eighteenth century, Father Fontecchio of the Society of Jesus planned a study of the superstitions and misinformation of the common people of Canton; in the preliminary outline he noted that the Fish was a shifting and shining creature that nobody had ever caught but that many said they had glimpsed in the depths of mirrors. Father Fontecchio died in 1736, and the work begun by his pen remained unfinished; some 150 years later Herbert Allen Giles took up the interrupted task. According to Giles, belief in the Fish is part of a larger myth that goes back to the legendary times of the Yellow Emperor.

In those days the world of mirrors and the world of men

were not, as they are now, cut off from each other. They were, besides, quite different; neither beings nor colours nor shapes were the same. Both kingdoms, the specular and the human, lived in harmony; you could come and go through mirrors. One night the mirror people invaded the earth. Their power was great, but at the end of bloody warfare the magic arts of the Yellow Emperor prevailed. He repulsed the invaders, imprisoned them in their mirrors, and forced on them the task of repeating, as though in a kind of dream, all the actions of men. He stripped them of their power and of their forms and reduced them to mere slavish reflections. Nonetheless, a day will come when the magic spell will be shaken off.

The first to awaken will be the Fish. Deep in the mirror we will perceive a very faint line and the colour of this line will be like no other colour. Later on, other shapes will begin to stir. Little by little they will differ from us; little by little they will not imitate us. They will break through the barriers of glass or metal and this time will not be defeated. Side by side with these mirror creatures, the creatures of water will join the battle.

In Yunnan they do not speak of the Fish but of the Tiger of the Mirror. Others believe that in advance of the invasion we will hear from the depths of mirrors the clatter of weapons.

Fauna of the United States

The yarns and tall tales of the lumber camps of Wisconsin and Minnesota include some singular creatures, in which, surely, no one ever believed.

There is the *Hidebehind*, which is always hiding behind

something. No matter how many times or whichever way a man turns, it is always behind him, and that's why nobody has been able to describe it, even though it is credited with having killed and devoured many a lumberjack.

Then there is the *Roperite*. This animal is about the size of a pony. It has a ropelike beak which it uses to snare even the fleetest of rabbits.

The *Teakettler* owes its name to the noises it makes, much like those of a boiling teakettle. Vaporous clouds fume from its mouth and it walks backward. It has been seen very few times.

The *Axehandle Hound* has a hatchet-shaped head, a handle-shaped body, and stumpy legs. This North Woods dachshund eats only the handles of axes.

Among the fish of this region we find the *Upland Trout*. They nest in trees and are good fliers but are scared of water.

There's another fish, the *Goofang*, that swims backward to keep the water out of its eyes. It's described as 'about the size of a sunfish, only much bigger'.

We shouldn't forget the *Goofus Bird* that builds its nest upside down and flies backward, not caring where it's going, only where it's been.

The *Gillygaloo* nested on the slopes of Paul Bunyan's famed Pyramid Forty, laying square eggs to keep them from rolling down the steep incline and breaking. These eggs were coveted by lumberjacks, who hard-boiled them and used them as dice.

And finally there's the *Pinnacle Grouse*, which had a single wing. This enabled it to fly in one direction only, circling the top of a conical hill. The colour of its plumage varied according to the season and according to the condition of the observer.

Garuda

Vishnu, second god of the triad that rules over the Hindu pantheon, rides either on the serpent that fills the seas or on the back of Garuda. Pictorially, Vishnu is represented as blue and with four arms, holding in each hand the club, the shell, the sphere, and the lotus. Garuda is half vulture and half man, with the wings, beak, and talons of the one and body and legs of the other. His face is white, his wings of a bright scarlet, and his body golden. Figures of Garuda, worked in bronze or stone, are worshipped in the temples of India. One is found in Gwalior, erected more than a hundred years before the Christian era by a Greek, Heliodorus, who became a follower of Vishnu.

In the *Garuda Purana* – one of the many *Puranas*, or traditions, of Hindu lore – Garuda expounds at length on the beginnings of the universe, the solar essence of Vishnu, the rites of his cult, the genealogies of the kings descended from the sun and the moon, the plot of the *Ramayana*, and various minor topics, such as the craft of verse, grammar, and medicine.

In a seventh-century drama called the *Mirth of the Snakes* and held to be the work of a king, Garuda kills and each day devours a snake (probably the hooded cobra) until a Buddhist prince teaches him the value of abstinence. In the last act, the penitent Garuda brings back to life the bones of the many generations of serpents he has fed upon. Eggeling holds that this work may be a Brahman satire on Buddhism.

Nimbarka, a mystic whose date is uncertain, has written that Garuda is a soul saved forever, as are his crown, his earrings, and his flute.

70

The Gnomes

The Gnomes are older than their name, which is Greek but which was unknown to the ancients, since it dates from the sixteenth century, Etymologists attribute it to the Swiss alchemist Paracelsus in whose writings it appears for the first time.

They are sprites of the earth and hills. Popular imagination pictures them as bearded dwarfs of rough and grotesque features; they wear tight-fitting brown clothes with monastic hoods. Like the griffons of Greece and of the East and the dragons of Germanic lore, the Gnomes watch over hidden treasure.

Gnosis, in Greek, means knowledge; and Paracelsus may have called them Gnomes because they know the exact places where precious metals are to be found.

The Golem

In a book inspired by infinite wisdom, nothing can be left to chance, not even the number of words it contains or the order of the letters; this is what the Kabbalists thought, and they devoted themselves to the task of counting, combining, and permutating the letters of the Scriptures, fired by a desire to penetrate the secrets of God. Dante stated that every passage of the Bible has a fourfold meaning – the literal, the allegorical, the moral, and the spiritual. Johannes Scotus Erigena, closer to the concept of divinity, had already said that the meanings of the Scriptures are infinite, like the hues in a peacock's tail. The Kabbalists would have approved this view; one of the secrets they sought in the Bible was how to create living beings. It was said of demons that they could make large and bulky creatures like the camel, but were incapable of creating anything delicate or frail, and Rabbi Eliezer denied them the ability to produce anything smaller than a barley grain. 'Golem' was the name given to the man created by combinations of letters; the word means, literally, a shapeless or lifeless clod.

In the Talmud (Sanhedrin, 65b) we read:

> If the righteous wished to create a world, they could do so. By trying different combinations of the letters of the ineffable names of God, Raba succeeded in creating a man, whom he sent to Rabbi Zera. Rabbi Zera spoke to him, but as he got no answer, he said: 'You are a creature of magic; go back to your dust.'

> Rabbi Hanina and Rabbi Oshaia, two scholars, spent every Sabbath eve studying the Book of Creation, by means of which they brought into being a three-year-old calf that they then used for the purposes of supper.

Schopenhauer, in his book *Will in Nature*, writes (Chapter 7): 'On page 325 of the first volume of his *Zauberbibliothek* [Magic Library], Horst summarizes the teachings of the English mystic Jane Lead in this way: Whoever possesses magical powers can, at will, master and change the mineral, vegetable, and animal kingdoms; consequently, a few magicians, working in agreement, could make this world of ours return to the state of Paradise.'

The Golem's fame in the West is owed to the work of the Austrian writer Gustav Meyrink, who in the fifth chapter of his dream novel *Der Golem* (1915) writes:

> It is said that the origin of the story goes back to the seventeenth century. According to lost formulas of the Kabbalah, a rabbi [Judah Loew ben Bezabel] made an artificial man — the aforesaid Golem — so that he would

ring the bells and take over all the menial tasks of the synagogue.

He was not a man exactly, and had only a sort of dim, half-conscious, vegetative existence. By the power of a magic tablet which was placed under his tongue and which attracted the free sidereal energies of the universe, this existence lasted during the daylight hours.

One night before evening prayer, the rabbi forgot to take the tablet out of the Golem's mouth, and the creature fell into a frenzy, running out into the dark alleys of the ghetto and knocking down those who got in his way, until the rabbi caught up with him and removed the tablet.

At once the creature fell lifeless. All that was left of him is the dwarfish clay figure that may be seen today in the New Synagogue.

Eleazar of Worms has preserved the secret formula for making a Golem. The procedures involved cover some twenty-three folio columns and require knowledge of the 'alphabets of the 221 gates', which must be recited over each of the Golem's organs. The word *Emet*, which means 'Truth', should be marked on its forehead; to destroy the creature, the first letter must be obliterated, forming the word *met*, whose meaning is 'death'.

The Griffon

Winged monsters, says Herodotus of the Griffons in his accounts of their continual warfare with the one-eyed Arimaspians; almost as sketchy, Pliny speaks of their long ears and hooked bills, yet judges them 'meere fables' (X, 49). Perhaps the most detailed description of the Griffon comes from the problematic Sir John Mandeville in Chapter 85 of his famous *Travels*:

> From this land men shal go unto the land of Bactry, where are many wicked men & fell, in that land are trees that beare wol, as it were shepe, of which they make cloth. In this land are ypotains [hippopotamuses] that dwel sometime on land, sometime on water, and are halfe a man and halfe a horse, and they eate not but men, when they may get them. In this land are many gryffons, more than in other places, and some say they haue the body before as an Egle, and behinde as a Lyon, and it is trouth, for they be made so; but the Griffen hath a body greater than viii Lyons and stall worthier than a hundred Egles. For certainly he wyl beare to his nest flying, a horse and a man upon his back, or two Oxen yoked togither as they go at plowgh, for he hath large nayles on hys fete, as great as it were hornes of Oxen, and of those they make cups there to drynke of, and of his rybes they make bowes to shoote with.

In Madagascar, another famous traveller, Marco Polo, heard the rukh spoken of and at first understood this as a reference to the *uccello grifone*, the Griffon bird (*Travels*, III, 36).

In the Middle Ages, the symbolism of the Griffon is contradictory. An Italian bestiary says that it stands for the Devil; usually it is an emblem of Christ, and this is how Isidore of Seville explains it in his *Etymologies*: 'Christ is a lion because he reigns and has great strength; and an eagle because, after the Resurrection, he ascended to heaven.'

In Canto XXIX of the *Purgatorio*, Dante has a vision of a triumphal chariot (the Church) drawn by a Griffon; its eagle portion is golden, its lion portion white mixed with red in order to signify – according to the commentaries – Christ's human nature. (White slightly reddened gives the colour of human flesh.) The commentators are recalling the description of the beloved in the Song of Solomon (V: 10–11): 'My beloved *is* white and ruddy ... His head *is as* the most fine gold ...'

Others feel that Dante wished to symbolize the Pope, who is both priest and king. Didron, in his *Manuel d'iconographie chrétienne* (1845), writes: 'The pope, as pontiff or eagle, is borne aloft to the throne of God to receive his commands, and as lion or king walks on earth with strength and might.'

Haniel, Kafziel, Azriel, and Aniel

In Babylon, the prophet Ezekiel saw in a vision four beasts or angels, 'And every one had four faces, and every one had four wings' and 'As for the likeness of their faces, they four had the face of a man, and the face of a lion, on the right side: and they four had the face of an ox on the left side; they four also had the face of an eagle.' They went where the spirit carried them, 'every one straight forward', or as the first Spanish Bible (1569) has it, *cada uno caminaua enderecho de su rostro* ('each one went in the direction of his face') which of course is so unimaginable as to be uncanny. Four wheels or rings, 'so high that they were dreadful' went with the angels and '*were* full of eyes round about them ...'

An echo from Ezekiel may have been in the mind of St John the Divine when he spoke of animals in the fourth chapter of Revelations:

> And before the throne *there was* a sea of glass like unto crystal: and in the midst of the throne, and round about the throne, *were* four beasts full of eyes before and behind.

And the first beast *was* like a lion, and the second beast like a calf, and the third beast had a face as a man, and the fourth beast *was* like a flying eagle.

And the four beasts had each of them six wings about *him*; and *they were* full of eyes within: and they rest not day and night, saying, Holy, holy, holy, Lord God Almighty, which was, and is, and is to come.

In the most important of Kabbalistic works, the *Zohar* or *Book of Splendour*, we read that these four beasts are called Haniel, Kafziel, Azriel, and Aniel and that they face east, north, south, and west. Stevenson remarked that if such beings were to be found in Heaven, what might not be expected of Hell.

A beast full of eyes is sufficiently awful, but Chesterton went further in the poem 'A Second Childhood':

But I shall not grow too old to see
   Enormous night arise,
A cloud that is larger than the world
And a monster made of eyes.

The fourfold angels in Ezekiel are called *Hayoth*, or Living Beings; according to the *Sefer Yeçirah*, another of the Kabbalist books, they are the ten numbers that were used by God, together with the twenty-two letters of the alphabet, to create the world; according to the *Zohar*, they came down from Heaven crowned with letters.

The Evangelists drew their symbols from the four faces of the *Hayoth*: to Matthew fell the man's face, sometimes bearded; to Mark, the lion's; to Luke, the calf's; and to John, the eagle's. St Jerome in his commentary on Ezekiel has attempted to reason out these attributions. Matthew was given the man's face because he emphasized the humanity of Christ; Mark the lion's because he declared Christ's royal standing; Luke the calf's because it is an emblem of sacrifice; John the eagle's because of Christ's soaring spirit.

A German scholar, Dr Richard Hennig, looks for the remote origin of these symbols in four zodiacal signs which lie ninety degrees apart. The lion and the calf give no trouble; the man has been linked to Aquarius, who has a man's face; and the eagle is evidently Scorpio, considered an ill omen and therefore changed. Nicholas de Vore, in his *Encylopedia of Astrology*, sustains the same hypothesis and remarks that the four figures come together in the sphinx, which may have a human head, the body of a bull, the claws and tail of a lion, and the wings of an eagle.

Haokah, the Thunder God

Among the Dakota Sioux, Haokah used the wind as sticks to beat the thunder drum. His horned head also marked him as a hunting god. He wept when he was happy and laughed in his sadness; heat made him shiver and cold made him sweat.

Harpies

In Hesiod's *Theogony*, the Harpies are winged divinities who wear long loose hair and are swifter than the birds and winds; in the *Aeneid* (Book III), they are vultures with a woman's face, sharp curved claws and filthy underparts, and are weak with a hunger they cannot appease. They swoop down from the mountains and plunder tables laid for feasts. They are invulnerable and emit an infectious smell; they gorge all they see, screeching the whole while and fouling everything with excrement. Servius, in his commentaries on Virgil, writes that just as Hecate is Proserpina in hell, Diana on earth, and Luna in heaven, and is called a threefold goddess, so the Harpies are Furies in hell, Harpies on earth, and Dirae (or Demons) in heaven. They are also confused with the Parcae, or Fates.

By order of the gods, the Harpies harried a Thracian king who unveiled men's futures, or who bought a long life with the price of his eyes, for which he was punished by the sun, whose works he had insulted by choosing blindness. He had prepared a banquet for all his court and the Harpies contaminated and devoured the dishes. The Argonauts put the Harpies to flight; Apollonius of Rhodes and William Morris (*The Life and Death of Jason*) tell the fantastic story. Ariosto in Canto XXXIII of the *Furioso* transforms the Thracian king into Prester John, fabled emperor of the Abyssinians.

Harpy comes from the Greek *harpazein* to snatch or carry away. In the beginning they were wind goddesses, like the Maruts of Vedic myth, who wielded weapons of gold (the lightning) and milked the clouds.

The Heavenly Cock

According to the Chinese, the Heavenly Cock is a golden-plumed fowl that crows three times a day. The first, when the sun takes its morning bath on the horizons of the sea; the second, when the sun is at its height; the last, when it sinks in the west. The first crowing shakes the heavens and stirs mankind from sleep. Among the offspring of the Cock is the *yang*, the male principle of the universe. The Cock has three legs and perches in the *fu-sang* tree, which grows in the lands of sunrise and whose height is measured by thousands of feet. The Heavenly Cock's crowing is very loud, and its bearing, lordly. It lays eggs out of which are hatched chicks with red combs, who answer his song every morning. All the roosters on earth are descended from the Heavenly Cock, whose other name is the Bird of Dawn.

The Hippogriff

To signify impossibility or incongruence, Virgil spoke of breeding horses with griffons. Four centuries later, his commentator Servius explained that the griffon is an animal which in the top half of its body is an eagle and in the bottom half a lion. To strengthen his text he added that they detest horses. In time, the expression *Jungentur jam grypes equis* ('To cross griffons with horses') came to be proverbial; at the beginning of the sixteenth century, Ludovico Ariosto, remembering it, invented the Hippogriff. Eagle and lion are united in the griffon of the ancients; horse and griffon in Ariosto's Hippogriff, which makes it a second generation monster or invention. Pietro Micheli notes that it is more harmonious than the winged horse Pegasus.

A detailed description of the Hippogriff, written as for a handbook of fantastic zoology, is given in *Orlando Furioso* (IV, 18):

> The steed is not imagined but real, for it was sired by a Griffon out of a mare: like its father's were its feathers and wings, its forelegs, head, and beak; in all its other parts it resembled its mother and was called Hippogriff; they come, though rarely, from the Rhiphaean Mountains, far beyond the icebound seas.

79

The first mention of the strange beast is deceptively casual (II, 37):

And by the Rhone I came upon a man in arms, reining in a great winged horse.

Other stanzas give us the wonder of this creature that flies. The following (IV, 4) is well known:

E vede l'oste e tutta la famiglia,
E chi a finestre e chi fuor ne la via,
Tener levati al ciel gli occhi e le ciglia,
Come l'Ecclisse o la Cometa sia.
Vede la Donna un'alta maraviglia,
Che di leggier creduta non saria:
Vede passar un gran destriero alato,
Che porta in aria un cavalliero armato.

[And she saw the landlord and all his house, and some at the windows and some in the street, their eyes and brows lifted to the sky as though it were an Eclipse or Comet. The Lady saw a wonder on high not easily to be believed: she saw pass over a great winged steed, bearing through the air a knight in arms.]

Astolpho, in one of the last cantos, unsaddles and unbridles the Hippogriff and sets it free.

Hochigan

Ages ago, a certain South African bushman, Hochigan, hated animals, which at that time were endowed with speech. One day he disappeared, stealing their special gift. From then on, animals have never spoken again.

Descartes tells us that monkeys could speak if they wished to, but that they prefer to keep silent so that they won't be made to work. In 1907, the Argentine writer Lugones published a story about a chimpanzee who was taught how to speak and died under the strain of the effort.

Humbaba

What was the giant Humbaba like, who guards the mountain cedars in that pieced-together Assyrian epic *Gilgamesh*, which may be the world's oldest poem? Georg Burckhardt has attempted to reconstruct it, and from his German version, published in Wiesbaden in 1952, we give this passage:

> Enkidu swung his axe and cut down one of the cedars. An angry voice rang out: 'Who has entered my forest and cut down one of my trees?' Then they saw Humbaba himself coming: he had the paws of a lion and a body covered with horny scales; his feet had the claws of a vulture, and on his head were the horns of a wild bull; his tail and male member each ended in a snake's head.

In one of the later cantos of *Gilgamesh*, we are introduced to creatures called Men-Scorpions who stand guard at the gate of the mountain Mashu. 'Its twin peaks [in an English version by N. K. Sandars] are as high as the wall of heaven and its paps reach down to the underworld.' It is into this mountain that the sun goes down at night and from which it returns at dawn. The Man-Scorpion is human in the upper part of its body, while its lower part ends in a scorpion's tail.

The Hundred-Heads

The Hundred-Heads is a fish created by a hundred ill-tempered words uttered in the course of an otherwise blameless life. A Chinese biography of the Buddha tells that he once met some fishermen who were dragging in a net. After much toil they hauled up on to the shore a huge fish with one head of an ape, another of a dog, another of a horse, another of a fox, another of a hog, another of a tiger, and so on, up to one hundred. The Buddha asked the fish:

'Are you Kapila?'

'Yes, I am,' the Hundred-heads answered before dying.

The Buddha explained to his disciples that in a previous incarnation Kapila was a Brahman who had become a monk and whose knowledge of the holy texts was unrivalled. Upon occasion, when his fellow students misread a word, Kapila would call them ape-head, dog-head, horse-head, and so forth. After his death, the karma of those many insults caused him to be reborn as a sea monster, weighed down by all the heads he had bestowed upon his companions.

The Hydra of Lerna

Typhon (the misshapen son of Tartarus and Terra) and Echidna, who was half beautiful woman and half serpent, gave birth to the Hydra of Lerna. Lemprière tells us that 'It had 100 heads, according to Diodorus; fifty according to Simonides; and nine according to the more received opinion of Apollodorus, Hyginus &c.' But what made the creature still more awful was that as soon as one of its heads was cut off, two more sprouted up in their place. It was said that the heads were human and that the middle one was everlasting. The Hydra's breath poisoned the waters and turned the fields brown. Even when it slept, the pollution in the air surrounding it could cause a man's death. Juno fostered the Hydra in her efforts to lessen Hercules' fame.

This monster appears to have been destined for eternity. Its den lay among the marshes near the lake of Lerna. Hercules and Iolaus went in search of it; Hercules lopped its heads and Iolaus applied a burning iron to the bleeding wounds, for only fire would stop the growth of the new heads. The last head, which was deathless, Hercules buried under a great boulder, and where it was buried it remains to this day, hating and dreaming.

In succeeding tasks with other beasts, Hercules inflicted deadly wounds with arrows dipped in the gall of the Hydra.

A sea crab friendly to the Hydra nipped Hercules' heel when he stepped on it during his struggle with the many-headed monster. Juno placed the crab in the heavens where it is now a constellation and the sign of Cancer.

Ichthyocentaurs

Lycophron, Claudian, and the Byzantine grammarian John Tzetzes have each at some time referred to the Ichthyocentaur; there are no other allusions to it in classical writings. Ichthyocentaur may be translated as 'Centaur-Fish'. The word is applied to beings that mythologists have also called Centaur-Tritons. The image abounds in Greek and Roman sculpture. They are human down to their waist, with the tail of a dolphin, and have the forelegs of a horse or a lion. Their place is among the gods of the ocean, close to the sea horses.

Jewish Demons

Between the world of the flesh and the world of the spirit, Jewish superstition imagined a middle ground inhabited by angels and devils. A census of its population left the bounds of arithmetic far behind. Throughout the centuries, Egypt, Babylonia, and Persia all enriched this teeming middle world. Maybe because of Christian influence (suggests Trachtenberg), demonology, or the lore of devils, became of less account than angelology, or the lore of angels.

Let us, however, single out Keteb Mereri, Lord of the Noontide and of Scorching Summers. Some children on their way to school once met up with him; all but two died. During the thirteenth century Jewish demonology swelled its ranks with Latin, French, and German intruders who ended up becoming thoroughly integrated with the natives recorded in the Talmud.

The Jinn

According to Moslem tradition, Allah created three different species of intelligent beings: Angels, who are made of light; Jinn ('Jinnee' or 'Genie' in the singular), who are made of fire; and Men, who are made of earth. The Jinn were created of a black smokeless fire some thousands of years before Adam, and consist of five orders. Among these orders we find good Jinn and evil, male Jinn and female. The cosmographer al-Qaswini says that 'the Jinn are aerial animals, with transparent bodies, which can assume various forms'. At first they may show themselves as clouds or as huge undefined pillars; when their form becomes condensed, they become visible, perhaps in the bulk of a man, a jackal, a wolf, a lion, a scorpion, or a snake. Some are true believers; others, heretics or atheists. The English Orientalist Edward William Lane writes that when Jinn take the shape of human beings they are sometimes of an enormously gigantic size and 'if good, they are generally resplendently handsome: if evil, horribly hideous.' They are also said to become invisible at pleasure 'by a rapid extension or rarefaction of the particles which compose them', when they may disappear into the air or earth or through a solid wall.

The Jinn often attain the lower heavens, where they overhear the conversations of angels about future events. This enables them to help wizards and soothsayers. Certain scholars attribute to them the building of the Pyramids or, under the orders of Solomon, the great Temple of Jerusalem.

The usual dwelling-places of Jinn are ruined houses, water cisterns, rivers, wells, crossroads, and markets. The Egyptians say that the pillarlike whirlwinds of sand raised in the desert are caused by the flight of an evil Jinnee. They also say that shooting stars are arrows hurled by Allah against evil Jinn. Among the acts perpetrated by these evil-doers against human beings, the following are traditional: the throwing of bricks and stones at passers-by from roofs and windows, the abduction of beautiful women, the persecution of anyone who tries to live in an uninhabited house, and the pilfering of provisions. Invoking the name of Allah the All Merciful, the Compassionate, is usually enough to secure one against such depredations, however.

The ghoul, which haunts burial grounds and feeds upon

dead human bodies, is thought to be an inferior order of the Jinn. Iblis is the father of the Jinn and their chief.

In 1828, young Victor Hugo wrote a tumultuous fifteen-stanza poem 'Les Djinns' about a gathering of these beings. With each stanza, as the Jinn cluster together, the lines grow longer and longer, until the eighth, when they reach their fullness. From this point on they dwindle to the close of the poem, when the Jinn vanish.

Burton and Noah Webster link the word 'Jinn' and the Latin 'genius', which is from the verb 'beget'. Skeat contradicts this.

The Kami

In a passage from Seneca, we read that Thales of Miletus taught that the earth floats in a surrounding sea, like a ship, and that these waters when tossed and driven by the tempests are the cause of earthquakes. Historians or mythologists of eighth-century Japan offer us a rather different seismological system. In the Sacred Scriptures it is written:

> Now beneath the Fertile-Land-of-Reed-Plains lay a Kami in the form of a great cat-fish, and by its movement it caused the earth to quake, till the Great Deity of Deer-Island thrust his sword deep into the earth and transfixed the Kami's head. So, now, when the evil Kami is violent, he puts forth his hand and lays it upon the sword till the Kami becomes quiet.

The hilt of this sword, carved in granite, projects some three feet out of the ground near the shrine of Kashima. In the seventeenth century, a feudal lord dug for six days without reaching the tip of the blade.

In popular belief, the *Jinshin-Uwo*, or Earthquake-Fish, is an eel seven hundred miles long that holds Japan on its back. It runs from north to south, its head lying beneath Kyoto and its tail beneath Awomori. Some logical thinkers have argued for the reverse of this order, for it is in the south of Japan that earthquakes are more frequent, and it is easier to equate this with the lashing of the eel's tail. This animal is not unlike the Bahamut of Moslem tradition or the Miðgarðsormr of the Eddas.

In certain regions the Earthquake-Fish is replaced, with little apparent advantage, by the Earthquake-Beetle (*Jinshin-Mushi*). It has a dragon's head, ten spider legs, and a scaly body. It is an underground, not an undersea, creature.

A King of Fire and His Steed

Heraclitus taught us that the primal element, or root, is fire, but this hardly means that there are beings made of fire, carved of the shifting substance of flames. This almost unimaginable fancy was attempted by William Morris in the tale 'The Ring Given to Venus' from his cycle *The Earthly Paradise* (1868–70). It runs as follows:

> Most like a mighty king was he,
> And crowned and sceptred royally;
> As a white flame his visage shone,
> Sharp, clear-cut as a face of stone;
> But flickering flame, not flesh, it was;
> And over it such looks did pass
> Of wild desire, and pain, and fear,
> As in his people's faces were,
> But tenfold fiercer: furthermore,

A wondrous steed the master bore,
Unnameable kind or make,
Not horse, nor hippogriff, nor drake.
Like and unlike to all of these,
And flickering like the semblances
Of an ill dream . . .

Perhaps in the above lines there is an echo of the deliberately ambiguous personification of Death in *Paradise Lost* (II, 666–73):

The other shape,
If shape it might be call'd that shape had none
Distinguishable in member, joint, or limb,
or substance might be call'd that shadow seem'd,
For each seem'd either; black it stood as Night,
Fierce as ten Furies, terrible as Hell,
And shook a dreadful Dart; what seem'd his head
The likeness of a Kingly Crown had on.

The Kraken

The Kraken is a Scandinavian version of the zaratan and of the sea dragon, or sea snake, of the Arabs.

In 1752–54, the Dane Erik Pontoppidan, Bishop of Bergen, published a *Natural History of Norway*, a work famous for its hospitality or gullibility. In its pages we read that the Kraken's back is a mile and a half wide and that its tentacles are capable of encompassing the largest of ships. The huge back protrudes from the sea like an island. The Bishop formulates this rule: 'Floating islands are invariably Krakens.' He also writes that the Kraken is in the habit of turning the sea murky with a discharge of liquid. This statement has inspired the hypothesis that the Kraken is an enlargement of the octopus.

Among Tennyson's juvenilia we find this poem to the curious creature:

The Kraken

Below the thunders of the upper deep,
Far, far beneath the abysmal sea,
His ancient, dreamless, uninvaded sleep
The Kraken sleepeth: faintest sunlights flee
About his shadowy sides; above him swell
Huge sponges of millennial growth and height;
And far away into the sickly light,
From many a wondrous grot and secret cell
Unnumber'd and enormous polypi
Winnow with giant arms the slumbering green.
There hath he lain for ages, and will lie
Battening upon huge sea-worms in his sleep,
Until the latter fire shall heat the deep;
Then once by man and angels to be seen,
In roaring he shall rise and on the surface die.

Kujata

In Moslem cosmology, Kujata is a huge bull endowed with four thousand eyes, ears, nostrils, mouths, and feet. To get from one ear to another or from one eye to another, no more than five hundred years are required. Kujata stands on the back of the fish Bahamut; on the bull's back is a great rock of ruby, on the rock an angel, and on the angel rests our earth. Under the fish is a mighty sea, under the sea a vast abyss of air, under the air fire, and under the fire a serpent so great that were it not for fear of Allah, this creature might swallow up all creation.

The Lamed Wufniks

There are on earth, and always were, thirty-six righteous men whose mission is to justify the world before God. They are the Lamed Wufniks. They do not know each other and are very poor. If a man comes to the knowledge that he is a Lamed Wufnik, he immediately dies and somebody else, perhaps in another part of the world, takes his place. Lamed Wufniks are, without knowing it, the secret pillars of the universe. Were it not for them, God would annihilate the whole of mankind. Unawares, they are our saviours.

This mystical belief of the Jews can be found in the works of Max Brod. Its remote origin may be the eighteenth chapter of Genesis, where we read this verse: 'And the Lord said, If I find in Sodom fifty righteous within the city, then I will spare all the place for their sakes.'

The Moslems have an analogous personage in the Kutb.

The Lamias

According to the Greeks and Romans, Lamias lived in Africa. From the waist up their form was that of a beautiful woman; from the waist down they were serpents. Many authorities thought of them as witches; others as evil monsters. They lacked the ability to speak, but they made a whistling sound which was musical, and in the spaces of the desert beguiled travellers in order to devour them. Their remote origin was divine, having sprung from one of the many loves of Zeus. In that section of his *Anatomy of Melancholy* (1621) that deals with the power of love, Robert Burton writes:

> *Philostratus*, in his Fourth Book *de vita Apollonii*, hath a memorable instance in this kind, which I may not omit, of one *Menippus Lycius* a young man 25 years of age, that going betwixt *Cenchreoe* and *Corinth*, met such a phantasm in the habit of a fair gentlewoman, which, taking him by the hand, carried him home to her house in the suburbs of *Corinth*, and told him she was a *Phoenician* by birth, and if he would tarry with her, *he should hear her sing and play, and drink such wine as never any drank, and no man should molest him; but she being fair and lovely would live and die with him, that was fair and lovely to behold.* The young man, a Philosopher, otherwise staid and discreet, able to moderate his passions, though not this of love, tarried with her a while to his great content, and at last married her, to whose wedding, among other guests, came *Apollonius*, who by some probable conjectures found her out to be a serpent, a *Lamia*, and that all her furniture was like *Tantalus'* gold described by *Homer*, no substance, but mere illusions. When she saw herself descried, she wept, and desired *Apollonius* to be silent, but he would not be moved, and thereupon she, plate, house, and all that was in it, vanished in an instant: *many thousands took notice of this fact, for it was done in the midst of Greece.*

Shortly before his death, John Keats was moved by this reading of Burton to compose his extensive poem 'Lamia'.

Laudatores Temporis Acti

The seventeenth-century Portuguese sea captain, Luiz da Silveira, in his *De Gentibus et Moribus Asiae* (Lisbon, 1669) refers somewhat obliquely to an Eastern sect – whether Indian or Chinese we are not told – which he calls, using a Latin tag, *Laudatores Temporis Acti*. The good captain is no metaphysician or theologian, but he none the less makes clear the nature of time past as conceived by the Worshippers. The past to us is merely a section of time, or a series of sections that were once the present and that may now be approximately recalled by memory or by history. Both memory and history make these sections, of course, part of the present. To the Worshippers, the past is absolute; it never had a present, nor can it be remembered or even guessed at. Neither unity nor plurality can be ascribed to it, since these are attributes of the present. The same may be said of its denizens – if the plural be allowed – with respect to their colour, size, weight, shape, and so on. Nothing about the beings of this Once That Never Was can be either affirmed or denied.

Silveira remarks on the utter hopelessness of the sect; the Past, as such, could have no inkling of its being worshipped and could afford no help or comfort to its votaries. Had the captain given us the native name or some other clue about this curious community, further investigation would be easier. We know they had neither temples nor sacred books. Are there still any Worshippers – or do they now, together with their dim belief, belong to the past?

The Lemures

The ancients supposed that men's souls after death wandered all over the world and disturbed the peace of its inhabitants. The good spirits were called *Lares familiares*, and the evil ones were known by the name of *Larvae*, or *Lemures*. They terrified the good, and continually haunted the wicked and impious; and the Romans had the custom of celebrating festivals in their honour, called *Lemuria*, or *Lemuralia*, in the month of May. They were first instituted by Romulus to appease the ghost of his brother Remus, from whom they were called *Remuria*, and, by corruption, *Lemuria*. These solemnities continued three nights, during which the temples of the gods were shut and marriages were prohibited. It was usual for the people to throw black beans on the graves of the deceased, or to burn them, as the smell was supposed to be insupportable to them. They also muttered magical words, and, by beating kettles and drums, they believed that the ghosts would depart and no longer come to terrify their relations upon earth.

LEMPRIÈRE: *Classical Dictionary*

The Leveller

Between 1840 and 1864, the Father of Light (whom we may also call the Inner Voice) granted the Bavarian musician and schoolteacher Jakob Lorber an unbroken series of trustworthy revelations concerning the human population, the fauna, and the flora of the celestial bodies of our solar system. Among the domestic animals we have knowledge of, thanks to these revelations, is found the Leveller, or Ground-Flattener (*Bodendrücker*), which renders immeasurable services on Miron, the planet identified with Neptune by Lorber's most recent editors.

The Leveller has ten times the girth of the elephant, to which it bears a striking resemblance. It is provided with a rather stumpy trunk and with long straight tusks; its hide is of a sickly green. Its limbs, pyramid-shaped, widen enormously at the hoof; the apexes of these pyramids appear to be pinned to the body. This noted plantigrade, in advance of builders and bricklayers, is led to the rough terrain of a construction site, where, with the aid of its hooves, its trunk, and its tusks, it proceeds to flatten out and tamp the ground.

The Leveller feeds on roots and herbage and has no enemies outside of one or two species of insects.

Lilith

'For before Eve was Lilith', we read in an old Hebrew text. This legend moved the English poet Dante Gabriel Rossetti (1828–82) to write the poem 'Eden Bower'. Lilith was a serpent; she was Adam's first wife and gave him

> Shapes that coiled in the woods and waters,
> Glittering sons and radiant daughters.

It was later that God created Eve; Lilith, to revenge herself on Adam's human wife, urged Eve to taste the forbidden fruit and to conceive Cain, brother and murderer of Abel. Such is the early form of the myth followed and bettered

Rossetti. Throughout the Middle Ages the influence of the word *layil*, Hebrew for 'night', gave a new turn to the myth. Lilith is no longer a serpent; she becomes an apparition of the night. At times she is an angel who rules over the procreation of mankind, at times a demon who assaults those who sleep alone or those who travel lonely roads. In popular imagination she is a tall silent woman with long black hair worn loose.

The Lunar Hare

In the blotches of the moon, the English believe they make out the form of a man; in *A Midsummer Night's Dream* there are two or three references to the 'man in the moon'. Shakespeare mentions its bundle, or bush, of thorn; in the last lines of Canto XX of the *Inferno*, Dante had already spoken of Cain and of these thorns. The commentary by Tommaso Casini cites the Tuscan fable in which the Lord banished Cain to the moon, condemning him to carry a bundle of thorns to the end of time. Others have seen in the moon the Holy Family; Leopoldo Lugones wrote in his *Lunario sentimental*:

> Y está todo: la Virgen con el niño; al flanco,
> San José (algunos tienen la buena fortuna
> De ver su vara); y el buen burrito blanco
> Trota que trota los campos de la luna.

[And everything is there: Virgin and Child; by her side, Saint Joseph (some are lucky enough to see his staff); and the good little white donkey that trots and trots over the acres of the moon.]

The Chinese speak of a Lunar Hare. Buddha, in one of his

former lives, suffered hunger; in order to feed him, a Hare leaped into a fire. The Buddha in gratitude sent the Hare's soul to the moon. There, under an acacia, the Hare pounds in a magical mortar the herbs that make up the elixir of life. In the common speech of certain provinces, this Hare is called the Physician or the Precious Hare or the Hare of Jade.

The ordinary Hare is believed to live for a thousand years and to turn white in its old age.

Shakespeare, by the way, refers to a dead mooncalf in *The Tempest* (II, ii). This creature, according to commentators, is an uncouth monster begotten on earth under the moon's influence.

The Mandrake

Like the barometz, the plant known as the Mandrake borders on the animal kingdom, since it gives a cry when it is torn up; this cry can drive those who hear it mad. We read in Shakespeare (*Romeo and Juliet*, IV, iii):

> And shrieks like mandrakes torn out of the earth,
> That living mortals, hearing them, run mad . . .

Pythagoras called the plant anthropomorphic; the Roman agronomist Lucius Columella called it semi-human; and Albertus Magnus wrote that the Mandrake is like man himself, down to the distinction between the sexes. Earlier, Pliny had said that the white Mandrake is the male and the black the female. Also, that those who root it out first trace three circles on the ground with a sword and look westward; the smell of its leaves is so strong that ordinarily it can deprive men of the power of speech. To uproot it was to run the risk of terrible calamities. In the last book of his *History of the*

Jewish Wars, Flavius Josephus advises us to employ a trained dog; the plant dug up, the dog dies, but the leaves are useful as a narcotic, a laxative, and for the purposes of magic.

The Mandrake's supposed human form has suggested the superstition that it grows at the foot of the gallows. Sir Thomas Browne (*Pseudodoxia Epidemica*, 1646) speaks of the grease of hanged men; the once popular German writer Hanns Heinz Ewers wrote a novel (*Alraune*, 1913) around the idea of the hanged man's seed being injected into a harlot and producing a beautiful witch. In German, 'mandrake' is *Alraune*; earlier it was *Alruna*, a word that comes originally from 'rune', which stood for 'whisper' or 'buzz'. Hence (according to Skeat) it meant 'a mystery . . . a writing, because written characters were regarded as a mystery known to the few'. Perhaps, more simply, the idea of a visible mark standing for a sound baffled the Nordic mind, and therein lay the mystery.

Genesis (XXX: 14–17) has this strange account of the reproductive powers of the Mandrake:

> And Reuben went in the days of wheat harvest, and found mandrakes in the field, and brought them unto his mother Leah. Then Rachel said to Leah, Give me, I pray thee, of thy son's mandrakes.
>
> And she said unto her, *Is it* a small matter that thou hast taken my husband? and wouldest thou take away my son's mandrakes also? And Rachel said, Therefore he shall lie with thee tonight for thy son's mandrakes.
>
> And Jacob came out of the field in the evening, and Leah went out to meet him, and said, Thou must come in unto me; for surely I have hired thee with my son's mandrakes. And he lay with her that night.
>
> And God hearkened unto Leah, and she conceived, and bare Jacob the fifth son.

In the twelfth century, a German-Jewish commentator on the Talmud wrote this paragraph:

A kind of cord comes out of a root in the ground and tied to the cord by its navel, like a squash or melon, is the animal known as the *yadu'a*, but the *yadu'a* is in all respects like a man: face, body, hands, and feet. It uproots and destroys all things around it as far as the cord reaches. The cord should be cut by an arrow, and the animal dies.

The physician Dioscorides (second century A.D.) identified the Mandrake with the *circea*, or herb of Circe, of which we read in the tenth book of the *Odyssey*:

At the root it was black, but its flower was like milk. Moly the gods call it, and it is hard for mortal man to dig; but the gods are all-powerful.

The Manticore

Pliny (VIII, 21) informs us that according to Ctesias, the Greek physician of Artaxerxes Mnemon, among the Ethiopians

there is a beast, which he calls Mantichora, hauing three ranks of teeth, which when they meet together, are let in one within another like the teeth of combs, with the face and eares of a man, with red eies, of colour sanguine, bodied like a Lion, and hauing a taile armed with a sting like a Scorpion: his voice resembles the noise of a flute and trumpet sounded together: very swift is he, and mans flesh of all other he chiefly desireth.

Flaubert has improved upon this description, and in the last pages of *The Temptation of Saint Anthony*, we read:

THE MANTICORE a gigantic red lion with a human face and three rows of teeth.

'The iridescence of my scarlet hide blends into the shimmering brightness of the desert sands. Through my nostrils I exhale the horror of the lonely places of the earth. I spite out pestilence. I consume armies when they venture into the desert.

'My nails are twisted into talons, like drills, and my teeth are cut like those of a saw; my restless tail prickles with darts, which I shoot left and right, before me, behind. Watch!'

The Manticore shoots the quills of its tail, which spread out like arrows on every hand. Drops of blood drip down, spattering the leaves of the trees.

The Mermecolion

The Mermecolion is an inconceivable animal defined by Flaubert in this way: 'lion in its foreparts, ant in its hindparts, with the organs of its sex the wrong way'. The history of this monster is also strange. In the Scriptures (Job IV, 11) we read: 'The old lion perisheth for lack of prey.' The Hebrew text has *layish* for lion; this word, an uncommon one for the lion, seems to have produced an equally uncommon translation. The Septuagint version, harking back to an Arabian lion that Aelian and Strabo call *myrmex*, forged the word Mermecolion. After centuries, the origin of this was forgotten. *Myrmex*, in Greek, means ant; out of the puzzling words 'The ant-lion perisheth for lack of prey' grew a fantasy (translated below by T. H. White) that medieval bestiaries succeeded in multiplying:

The Physiologus said: It had the face (or fore-part) of a lion and the hinder parts of an ant. Its father eats flesh,

99

but its mother grains. If then they engender the ant-lion, they engender a thing of two natures, such that it cannot eat flesh because of the nature of its mother, nor grains because of the nature of its father. It perishes, therefore, because it has no nutriment.

The Minotaur

The idea of a house built so that people could become lost in it is perhaps more unusual than that of a man with a bull's head, but both ideas go well together and the image of the labyrinth fits with the image of the Minotaur. It is equally fitting that in the centre of a monstrous house there be a monstrous inhabitant.

The Minotaur, half bull and half man, was born of the furious passion of Pasiphae, Queen of Crete, for a white bull that Neptune brought out of the sea. Daedalus, who invented the artifice that carried the Queen's unnatural desires to gratification, built the labyrinth destined to confine and keep hidden her monstrous son. The Minotaur fed on human flesh and for its nourishment the King of Crete imposed on the city of Athens a yearly tribute of seven young men and seven maidens. Theseus resolved to deliver his country from this burden when it fell to his lot to be sacrificed to the Minotaur's hunger. Ariadne, the King's daughter, gave him a thread so that he could trace his way out of the windings of the labyrinth's corridors; the hero killed the Minotaur and was able to escape from the maze.

Ovid in a line that is meant to be clever speaks of the *Semibovemque virum, semivirumque bovem* ('the man half bull, the bull half man'). Dante, who was familiar with the writings of the ancients but not with their coins or monuments, imagined the Minotaur with a man's head and a bull's body (*Inferno*, XII, 1–30).

The worship of the bull and of the two-headed axe (whose name was *labrys* and may have been at the root of the word *labyrinth*) was typical of pre-Hellenic religions, which held sacred bullfights. Human forms with bull heads figured, to judge by wall paintings, in the demonology of Crete. Most likely the Greek fable of the Minotaur is a late and clumsy version of far older myths, the shadow of other dreams still more full of horror.

The Monkey of the Inkpot

This animal, common in the north, is four or five inches long; its eyes are scarlet and its fur is jet black, silky, and soft as a pillow. It is marked by a curious instinct – the taste for India ink. When a person sits down to write, the monkey squats cross-legged near by with one forepaw folded over the other, waiting until the task is over. Then it drinks what is left of the ink, and afterwards sits back on its haunches, quiet and satisfied.

WANG TAI-HAI (1791)

The Monster Acheron

Only one person, one time, ever saw the monster Acheron; this took place in the twelfth century in the Irish town of Cork. The original version of the story, written in Gaelic, is now lost, but a Benedictine monk from Regensburg

(Ratisbon) translated it into Latin, and for this translation the tale passed into a number of languages, among them Swedish and Spanish. Of the Latin version there are some fifty-odd manuscripts extant, agreeing in all the essentials. *Visio Tundali* (Tundal's Vision) is the story's name, and it has been considered one of the sources of Dante's poem.

Let us begin with the word 'Acheron'. In the tenth book of the *Odyssey* it is one of the rivers of hell, flowing somewhere on the western borders of the inhabited world. Its name is re-echoed in the *Aeneid*, in Lucan's *Pharsalia*, and in Ovid's *Metamorphoses*. Dante engraves it in a line: *Su la trista riviera d'Acheronte* ('On the sad shores of the Acheron').

In one myth, Acheron is a Titan suffering punishment; in another, dating earlier, he is placed close to the South Pole, below the constellations of the antipodes. The Etruscans had 'books of fate' that taught divination and 'books of Acheron' that taught the ways of the soul after bodily death. In time, Acheron came to stand for hell.

Tundal was an Irish gentleman, well-mannered and brave, but of hardly irreproachable habits. He once fell ill while at the home of a lady friend, and for three days and nights was taken for dead, except for a bit of warmth in his heart. When he recovered his senses, he told that his guardian angel had shown him the lands beyond this world. Of the many wonders he saw, the one which interests us here is the monster Acheron.

He is bigger than any mountain. His eyes flame and his mouth is so large that nine thousand persons could fit in it. Two damned men, like pillars or atlantes, prop it open; one stands on his feet, the other on his head. Three throats lead inside and belch undying fire. From deep in the beast's belly comes the continuous wailing of the countless lost souls who are being devoured. Devils tell Tundal that the monster is called Acheron. His guardian angel deserts him, and Tundal is swept inside with the others. There he finds himself in the midst of tears, darkness, gnashing teeth, fire, unbearable burning, icy cold, dogs, bears, lions, and snakes. In this legend, hell is a beast with other beasts inside it.

In 1758, Emanuel Swedenborg wrote: 'It has not been granted me to perceive Hell's general shape, but I have been told that in the same way that Heaven has a human shape, Hell has the shape of a devil.'

The Mother of Tortoises

Twenty-two centuries before the Christian era, the good emperor Yü the Great travelled and measured with his steps the Nine Mountains, the Nine Rivers, and the Nine Marshes, and divided the land into Nine Provinces fit for virtue and agriculture. In this way he held back the Waters that threatened to flood Heaven and Earth, and left us this account of his Public Works (Legge's translation):

> I mounted my four conveyances (carts, boats, sledges, and spiked shoes), and all along the hills hewed down the woods, at the same time, along with Yi, showing the multitudes how to get flesh to eat. I opened passages for the streams throughout the nine provinces, and conducted them to the sea. I deepened the channels and canals, and conducted them to the streams, at the same time, along with Chi, sowing grain, and showing the multitudes how to procure the food of toil in addition to flesh meat.

Historians tell that the manner in which he divided his territory was revealed to him by a supernatural or sacred Tortoise that arose from the bed of a river. There are those who claim that this amphibious creature, the mother of all Tortoises, was made of water and fire; others attribute a less common substance to it: starlight of the constellation

Sagittarius. On the Tortoise's shell could be read a cosmic treatise called the *Hong Fan* (Universal Rule), or a diagram made of black and white dots of the Nine Subdivisions of that treatise.

To the Chinese, the heavens are hemispherical and the earth quadrangular, and so, in the Tortoise with its curved upper shell and flat lower shell, they find an image or model of the world. Moreover, Tortoises share in cosmic longevity; it is therefore fitting that they should be included among the spiritually endowed creatures (together with the unicorn, the dragon, the phoenix, and the tiger) and that soothsayers read the future in the pattern of their shells.

Than-Qui (Tortoise-Spirit) is the name of the creature that revealed the *Hong Fan* to the emperor.

The Nagas

Nagas belong to the mythology of India. They are serpents but often take the form of a man.

In one of the books of the *Mahabharata*, Arjuna is pursued by Ulupi, the daughter of a Naga king, and firmly but gently has to remind her of his vow of chastity; the maiden tells him that his duty lies in soothing the unhappy. The hero grants her a night. The Buddha, meditating under a fig tree, is chastised by the wind and the rain; a Naga out of pity coils itself around him in a sevenfold embrace and opens over him its seven heads so as to form a kind of umbrella. The Buddha converts him to the Faith.

Kern in his *Manual of Indian Buddhism*, speaks of the Nagas as cloudlike serpents. They live underground in deep palaces. Believers in the Greater Vehicle tell that the Buddha preached one law to mankind and another to the gods, and that this latter – the secret law – was kept in the heavens and palaces of the serpents, who revealed it centuries later to the monk Nagarjuna.

We give an Indian legend set down by the Chinese pilgrim Fa-hsien early in the fifth century:

> King Asoka came to a lake near whose edge stood a lofty pagoda. He thought of pulling it down in order to raise a higher one. A Brahman let him into the tower and once inside told him:
>
> 'My human form is an illusion. I am really a Naga, a dragon. My sins condemn me to inhabit this frightful body, but I obey the law preached by the Buddha and hope to work my redemption. You may pull down this shrine if you believe you can build a better one.'
>
> The Naga showed him the vessels of the altar. The king looked at them with alarm, for they were quite unlike those made by the hands of men, and he left the pagoda standing.

The Nasnas

Among the monstrous creatures of the *Temptation* is the Nasnas, which 'has only one eye, one cheek, one hand, one leg, half a torso and half a heart'. A commentator, Jean-Claude Margolin, credits the invention of this beast to Flaubert, but Lane in the first volume of *The Arabian Nights' Entertainments* (1839) says it is believed to be the offspring of the Shikk, a demonical creature divided longitudinally, and a human being. The Nasnas, according to Lane (who gives it as Nesnás), resembles 'half a human being; having half a head, half a body, one arm, and one leg, with which it hops with much agility ...' It is found in the woods and desert country of Yemen and Hadhramaut, and is endowed with speech. One race has its face in the breast, like the *blemies,* and a tail like that of a sheep. Its flesh is sweet and much sought after. Another variety of Nasnas, having the wings of a bat, inhabits the island of Ráïj (perhaps Borneo) at the edge of the China seas. 'But God,' adds the sceptical authority, 'is All-Knowing.'

The Norns

In medieval Norse mythology the Norns are the Fates. Snorri Sturluson, who at the beginning of the thirteenth century brought order to the scattered Northern myths, tells us that the Norns are three and that their names are Urth (the past), Verthandi (the present), and Skuld (the future). These three heavenly Norns ruled the fate of the world, while at the birth of every man three individual Norns were present, casting the weird of his life. It may be suspected that the names of the Norns are a refinement or addition of a theological nature; ancient Germanic tribes were incapable of such abstract thinking. Snorri shows us three maidens by a fountain at the base of the World Tree, Yggdrasil. Inexorably, they weave our fate.

Time (of which they are made) seemed to have quite forgotten them, but around 1606 William Shakespeare wrote the tragedy of *Macbeth,* in whose first scene they appear. They are the three witches who predict what fate holds in store for Banquo and Macbeth. Shakespeare calls them the weird sisters (I, iii):

The weird sisters, hand in hand,
Posters of the seas and land,
Thus do go about, about . . .

Wyrd among the Anglo-Saxons was the silent goddess who presided over the destiny of gods and men.

The Nymphs

Paracelsus limited their dominion to water, but the ancients thought the world was full of Nymphs. They distinguished them by names according to the palaces they haunted. The Dryads, or Hamadryads, dwelled in trees, without being seen, and died with them. Other Nymphs were held to be immortal or, as Plutarch obscurely intimates, lived for above 9,720 years. Among these were the Nereids and the Oceanids, which presided over the sea. Nymphs of the lakes and streams were Naiads; those of mountains and caves, Oreads. There were also Nymphs of the glens, called Napaeae, and of groves called Alseids. The exact number of the Nymphs is unknown; Hesiod gives us the figure three thousand. They were earnest young women and very beautiful; their name may mean simply 'marriageable woman'. Glimpsing them could cause blindness and, if they were naked, dead. A line of Propertius affirms this.

The ancients made them offerings of honey, olive oil, and milk. They were minor goddesses, but no temples were erected in their honour.

The Odradek

Some say the word Odradek is of Slavonic origin, and try to account for it on that basis. Others again believe it to be of German origin, only influenced by Slavonic. The uncertainty of both interpretations allows one to assume with justice that neither is accurate, especially as neither of them provides an intelligent meaning of the word.

No one, of course, would occupy himself with such studies if there were not a creature called Odradek. At first glance it looks like a flat star-shaped spool for thread, and indeed it does seem to have thread wound upon it; to be sure, they are only old, broken-off bits of thread, knotted and tangled together, of the most varied sorts and colours. But it is not only a spool, for a small wooden crossbar sticks out of the middle of the star, and another small rod is joined to that at a right angle. By means of this latter rod on one side and one of the points of the star on the other, the whole thing can stand upright as if on two legs.

One is tempted to believe that the creature once had some sort of intelligible shape and is now only a broken-down remnant. Yet this does not seem to be the case; at least there is no sign of it; nowhere is there an unfinished or unbroken surface to suggest anything of the kind; the whole thing looks senseless enough, but in its own way perfectly finished. In any case, closer scrutiny is impossible, since Odradek is extraordinarily nimble and can never be laid hold of.

He lurks by turns in the garret, the stairway, the lobbies, the entrance hall. Often for months on end he is not to be seen; then he has presumably moved into other houses; but he always comes faithfully back to our house again. Many a time when you go out of the door and he happens just to be leaning directly beneath you against the banisters you feel inclined to speak to him. Of course, you put no difficult questions to him, you treat him – he is so diminutive that you cannot help it – rather like a child. 'Well, what's your name?' you ask him. 'Odradek,' he says. 'And where do you live?' 'No fixed abode,' he says and laughs; but it is only the kind of laughter that has no lungs behind it. It sounds rather like the rustling of fallen leaves. And that is usually the end of the conversation. Even these answers are not always forthcoming; often he stays mute for a long time, as wooden as his appearance.

I ask myself, to no purpose, what is likely to happen to him? Can he possibly die? Anything that dies has had some kind of aim in life, some kind of activity, which has worn out; but that does not apply to Odradek. Am I to suppose, then, that he will always be rolling down the stairs, with ends of thread trailing after him, right before the feet of my children, and my children's children? He does no harm to anyone that one can see; but the idea that he is likely to survive me I find almost painful.

FRANZ KAFKA: *The Penal Colony*
(Translated from the German by
Willa and Edwin Muir)

[This piece was originally titled *Die Sorge des Hausvaters* – 'The Cares of a Family Man'.]

An Offspring of Leviathan

In the *Golden Legend*, a thirteenth-century compendium of lives of the saints written by the Dominican friar Jacobus de Voragine, read and re-read in the Middle Ages but now neglected, we find much curious lore. The book went through numerous editions and translations, among them the one into English printed by William Caxton. Chaucer's 'Second Nonne's Tale' has its source in the *Legenda aurea*; Longfellow also was inspired by the work of Jacobus, taking the title from the *Golden Legend* for one of the books of his trilogy *Christus*.

Out of Jacobus' medieval Latin, we translate the following from the chapter on St Martha (CV [100]):

> There was at that time, in a certain wood above the Rhone between Arles and Avignon, a dragon that was half beast and half fish, larger than an ox and longer than a horse. Armed with a pair of tusks that were like swords and pointed as horns, it lay in wait in the river, killing all wayfarers and swamping boats. It had come, however, from the sea of Galatia in Asia Minor and was begotten by Leviathan, the fiercest of all water serpents, and by the Wild Ass, which is common to those shores . . .

One-Eyed Beings

Before it became the name of an optical instrument, the word 'monocle' was applied to beings who had a single eye. So, in a sonnet composed at the beginning of the seventeenth century, Góngora writes of the *Monóculo galán de Gal-*

atea ('The monocle who yearns for Galatea') – referring, of course, to Polyphemus, of whom he had previously written in his *Fábula de Polifemo:*

Un monte era de miembros eminente
Este que, de Neptuno hijo fiero,
De un ojo ilustra el orbe de su frente,
Émulo casi del mayor lucero;
Cíclope a quien el pino más valiente
Bastón le obedecía tan ligero,
Y al grave peso junco tan delgado,
Que un día era bastón y otro caiado.

Negro el cabello, imitador undoso
De las oscuras aguas del Leteo,
Al viento que le peina proceloso
Vuela sin orden, pende sin aseo;
Un torrente es su barba impetuoso
Que, adusto hijo de este Pirineo,
Su pecho inunda, o tarde o mal o en vano
Surcada aún de los dedos de su mano.

[An eminent peak of limbs he was, this uncouth son of Neptune, lighting the orb of his forehead with an eye almost rivalling the greatest star; a Cyclops to whom the stoutest pine obeyed as a light cane, and was to his bulky mass a reed so slender that one day it was a walking-stick and the next a shepherd's crook.

Jet black his hair, a wavy imitator of the dark waters of the Lethe, in the wind which stormily combs it, blowing in a tangle and dangling in disorder; a plunging torrent is his beard, which – stern son of this Pyrenee – overflows his breast, too late or badly or in vain furrowed by the fingers of his hand.]

These lines outdo and are weaker than others from the third book of the *Aeneid* (praised by Quintilian), which in turn outdo and are weaker than still other lines from the ninth book of the *Odyssey*. This literary decline matches a decline in the poet's faith; Virgil wishes to impress us with his Polyphemus, but scarcely believes in him; and Góngora believes only in words or in verbal trickery.

The Cyclops were not the only race of men having one eye; Pliny (VII, 2) also mentions the Arimaspians,

> known by this marke, for hauing one eie only in the mids of their forehead: and these maintain war ordinarily about the mettall mines of gold, especially with griffons, a kind of wilde beasts that flie, and use to fetch gold out of the veines of those mines (as commonly it is receiued:) which sauage beasts . . . strive as eagerly to keepe and hold those golden mines, as the Arimaspians to disseize them thereof, and to get away the gold from them.

Five hundred years earlier, the first encyclopedist, Herodotus of Halicarnassus, had written (III, 116):

> This is also plain, that to the north of Europe there is by far more gold than elsewhere. In this matter again I cannot with certainty say how the gold is got; some will have it that one-eyed men called Arimaspians steal it from griffons. But this too I hold incredible, that there can be men in all else like other men, yet having but one eye.

The Panther

In medieval bestiaries the word 'panther' deals with a very different animal from the carnivorous mammal of present-day zoology. Aristotle had written that it gives off a sweet smell attractive to other animals; Aelian – the Roman author nicknamed 'Honey-Tongued' for his perfect command of Greek, a language he preferred to Latin – stated that this odour was also pleasant to men. (In this characteristic some see a confusion of the Panther with the civet cat.) Pliny endowed the Panther's back with a large circular spot that waxed and waned with the moon. To these marvellous circumstances came to be added the fact that the Bible, in the Septuagint version, uses the word 'panther' in a verse (Hosea, V: 14) that may be a prophetic reference to Jesus: 'I am become as a panther to Ephraim.'

In the Anglo-Saxon bestiary of the *Exeter Book*, the Panther is a gentle, solitary beast with a melodious voice and sweet breath (likened elsewhere to the smell of allspice) that makes its home in a secret den in the mountains. Its only foe is the dragon, with which it fights incessantly. After a full meal it sleeps and 'On the third day when he wakes, a lofty, sweet, ringing sound comes from his mouth, and with the song a most delightful stream of sweet-smelling breath, more grateful than all the blooms of herbs and blossoms of the trees.' Multitudes of men and animals flock to its den from the fields and castles and towns, drawn on by the fragrance and the music. The dragon is the age-old enemy, the Devil; the waking is the resurrection of the Lord; the multitudes are the community of the faithful; and the Panther is Jesus Christ.

To attenuate the amazement this allegory can awaken, let us remember that the Panther was not a wild beast to the Saxons but an exotic sound unsupported by any very concrete image. It may be added, as a curiosity, that Eliot's poem 'Gerontion' speaks of 'Christ the tiger'.

Leonardo da Vinci notes:

The African panther is like a lion, but with longer legs, and a more slender body. It is completely white, spattered with black spots like rosettes. Its beauty delights the other animals, which would all flock to it were it not for the panther's terrible stare. Aware of this, the panther lowers its eyes; other animals approach it to drink in such

beauty, and the panther pounces on the nearest of
them.

The Pelican

The Pelican of everyday zoology is a water bird with a wing-
span of some six feet and a very long bill whose lower man-
dible distends to form a pouch for holding fish. The Pelican
of fable is smaller and its bill is accordingly shorter and
sharper. Faithful to popular etymology – *pelicanus*, white-
haired – the plumage of the former is white while that of
the latter is yellow and sometimes green. (The real origin of
pelican is from the Greek 'I hew with an axe', in a confusion
of its large bill with that of the woodpecker's.) But more
unusual than its appearance are its habits.

With its bill and claws, the mother bird caresses her
offspring with such devotion that she kills them. After three
days the father arrives and, despairing over the deaths of his
young, rips at his own breast with his bill. The blood that
spills from his wounds revives the dead birds. This is the
account given in medieval bestiaries, though St Jerome in a
commentary on the 102nd Psalm ('I am like a pelican of the
wilderness: I am like an owl of the desert') attributes the
death of the nestlings to the serpent. That the Pelican opens
its breast and feeds its young with its own blood is the
common version of the fable.

Blood that gives life to the dead suggests the Eucharist and
the cross, and so a famous line of the *Paradiso* (XXV, 113)
calls Jesus Christ *nostro Pellicano* – mankind's Pelican. The
Latin commentary by Benvenuto of Imola amplifies this
point: 'He is called pelican because he opened his side for our
salvation, like the pelican that revives its dead brood with

the blood of its breast. The pelican is an Egyptian Bird.'

The Pelican is common in ecclesiastical heraldry and it is still engraved on chalices. The bestiary by Leonardo da Vinci describes the Pelican in this way:

It is greatly devoted to its young and, finding them in the nest killed by snakes, tears at its breast, bathing them with its blood to bring them back to life.

The Peryton

The Sibyl of Erythraea, it is said, foretold that the city of Rome would finally be destroyed by the Perytons. In the year A.D. 642 the record of the Sibyl's prophecies was consumed in the great conflagration of Alexandria; the grammarians who undertook the task of restoring certain charred fragments of the nine volumes apparently never came upon the special prophecy concerning the fate of Rome.

In time it was deemed necessary to find a source that would throw greater light upon this dimly remembered tradition. After many vicissitudes it was learned that in the sixteenth century a rabbi from Fez (in all likelihood Jakob Ben Chaim) had left behind a historical treatise in which he quoted the now lost work of a Greek scholiast, which included certain historical facts about the Perytons obviously taken from the oracles before the Library of Alexandria was burned by Omar. The name of the learned Greek has not come down to us, but his fragments run:

The Perytons had their original dwelling in Atlantis and are half deer, half bird. They have the deer's head and legs. As for its body, it is perfectly avian, with corresponding wings and plumage . . .

Its strangest trait is that, when the sun strikes it, instead of casting a shadow of its own body, it casts the shadow of a man. From this, some conclude that the Perytons are the spirits of wayfarers who have died far from their homes and from the care of their gods . . .

. . . and have been surprised eating dry earth . . . flying in flocks and have been seen at a dizzying height above the Columns of Hercules.

. . . they [Perytons] are mortal foes of the human race; when they succeed in killing a man, their shadow is that of their own body and they win back the favour of their gods.

. . . and those who crossed the seas with Scipio to conquer Carthage came close to failure, for during the passage a formation of Perytons swooped down on the ships, killing and mangling many . . . Although our weapons have no effect against it, the animal – if such it be – can kill no more than a single man.

. . . wallowing in the gore of its victims and then fleeing upward on its powerful wings.

. . . in Ravenna, where they were last seen, telling of their plumage which they described as light blue in colour, which greatly surprised me for all that is known of their dark green feathers.

Though these excerpts are sufficiently explicit, it is to be lamented that down to our own time no further intelligence about the Perytons has reached us. The rabbi's treatise, which preserved this description for us, had been on deposit until before the last World War in the library of the University of Dresden. It is painful to say that this document has also disappeared, and whether as a consequence of bombardment or of the earlier book burning of the Nazis, it is not known. Let us hope that one day another copy of the work may be discovered and again come to adorn the shelves of some library.

The Phoenix

In monumental effigies, in pyramids of stone, and in treasured mummies, the Egyptians sought eternity. It is therefore appropriate that their country should have given rise to the myth of a cyclical and deathless bird, though its subsequent elaboration is the work of Greece and of Rome. Adolf Erman writes that in the mythology of Heliopolis, the Phoenix (*benu*) is the lord of jubilees or of long cycles of time. Herodotus, in a famous passage (II, 73), tells with insistent scepticism an early form of the legend:

> Another bird also is sacred; it is called the phoenix. I myself have never seen it, but only pictures of it; for the bird comes but seldom into Egypt, once in five hundred years, as the people of Heliopolis say. It is said that the phoenix comes when his father dies. If the picture truly shows his size and appearance, his plumage is partly golden and partly red. He is most like an eagle in shape and bigness. The Egyptians tell a tale of this bird's devices which I do not believe. He comes, they say, from Arabia bringing his father to the Sun's temple enclosed in myrrh, and there buries him. His manner of bringing is this: first he moulds an egg of myrrh as heavy as he can carry, and when he has proved its weight by lifting it he then hollows out the egg and puts his father in it, covering over with more myrrh the hollow in which the body lies; so the egg being with his father in it of the same weight as before, the phoenix, after enclosing him, carries him to the temple of the Sun in Egypt. Such is the tale of what is done by this bird.

Some five hundred years later, Tacitus and Pliny took up the wondrous tale; the former justly observed that all antiquity is obscure, but that a tradition has fixed the intervals of the Phoenix's visits at 1,461 years (*Annals*, VI, 28). The latter also looked into the Phoenix's chronology; Pliny records (X, 2) that, according to Manilius, the bird's life coincides with the period of the Platonic year, or Great Year. A Platonic year is the time required by the sun, the moon, and the five planets to return to their initial position; Tacitus in his *Dialogus de Oratoribus* gives this as 12,994 common years. The ancients believed that, upon fulfilment of this vast astronomical cycle, the history of the world would repeat itself in all its details under the repeated influence of the planets; the Phoenix would be a mirror or an image of this process. For a closer analogy between the cosmos and the Phoenix, it should be recalled that, according to the Stoics, the universe dies in fire and is reborn in fire and that the cycle had no beginning and will have no end.

Time simplified the method of the Phoenix's generation. Herodotus speaks of an egg and Pliny of a maggot, but the poet Claudian at the end of the fourth century already celebrates an immortal bird that rises out of its own ashes, an heir to itself and a witness of the ages.

Few myths have been as widespread as that of the Phoenix. In addition to the authors already cited, we may add: Ovid (*Metamorphoses*, XV), Dante (*Inferno*, XXIV), Pellicer (*The Phoenix and its Natural History*), Quevedo (*Spanish Parnassus*, VI), and Milton (*Samson Agonistes, in fine*). Shakespeare at the close of *Henry VIII* (V, iv) wrote these fine verses:

> But as when
> The bird of wonder dies, the maiden phoenix,
> Her ashes new create another heir,
> As great in admiration as herself . . .

We may also mention the Latin poem 'De Arte Phoenice', which has been attributed to Lactantius, and an Anglo-Saxon imitation of it dating from the eighth century. Tertulius, St Ambrose, and Cyrillus of Jerusalem have used the Phoenix as a proof of the resurrection of the flesh. Pliny pokes fun at the physicians who prescribe pills compounded of the nest and ashes of the Phoenix.

The Pygmies

In the knowledge of the ancients, this nation of dwarfs – measuring twenty-seven inches in height – dwelled in the mountains beyond the utmost limits of India or of Ethiopia. Pliny states that they built their cabins of mud mixed with feathers and eggshells. Aristotle allots them underground dens. For the harvest of wheat they wielded axes, as though they were out to chop down a forest. Each year they were attacked by flocks of cranes whose home lay on the Russian steppe. Riding rams and goats, the Pygmies retaliated by destroying the eggs and nests of their foes. These expeditions of war kept them busy for the space of three months out of every twelve.

Pygmy was also the name of a Carthaginian god whose face was carved as a figurehead on warships in order to spread terror among the enemy.

The Rain Bird

When rain is needed, Chinese farmers have at their disposal – besides the dragon – the bird called the *shang yang*. It has only one leg. Long ago, children hopped up and down on one foot, wrinkling their brows and repeating: 'It will thunder, it will rain, 'cause the *shang yang*'s here again!' The tradition runs that the bird drew water from the rivers with its beak and blew it out as rain on the thirsting fields.

An ancient wizard had tamed it and used to carry it perched on his sleeve. Historians tell us that it once paraded back and forth before the throne of the Prince of Ch'i, hopping about and flapping its wings. The Prince, greatly taken aback, sent his chief minister to the Court of Lu to consult Confucius. The Sage foretold that the *shang yang* would cause the whole countryside and near-by regions to be flooded unless dikes and channels were built at once. The Prince was not deaf to the Sage's warning, and so in his domain countless damage and disaster were avoided.

The Remora

Remora, in Latin, means 'delay' or 'hindrance'. This is the strict meaning of the word which was figuratively applied to the *Echeneis*, a genus of sucking fishes credited with the power of holding a ship fast by clinging to it. The Remora is a fish of an ashen hue; on the top of its head it has a cartilaginous disc with which it creates a vacuum that enables it to cling to other underwater creatures. Here is Pliny's acclamation of its powers (IX, 25):

There is a very little fish keeping vsually about rocks, named Echeneis: it is thought, that if it settle and stick to the keele of a ship vnder water, it goeth the slower by that means: whereupon it was so called: and for that cause also it hath but a bad name in matters of loue, for inchanting as it were both men and women, and bereauing them of their heat and affection that way: as also in law cases, for delay of issues and iudicial trials. But both these imputations and slanders it recompenseth again with one good vertue and commendable quality that it hath: for in great bellied women if it can be applied outwardly it stayeth the dangerous flux of the womb, and holds the child vnto the full time of birth: howbeit it is not allowed for meat to be eaten. *Aristotle* thinketh, that it hath a number of feet, the fins stand so thick one by another.

(Pliny goes on to describe the murex, a variety of purple fish also credited with bringing ships under full sail to a standstill; then, returning to the 'Stay-Ship Echeneis', he reports that 'it is a foot long, and fiue fingers thicke, and that oftentimes it stayeth a ship. And moreouer ... it hath this vertue being kept in salt, to draw vp gold that is fallen into a pit or well being neuer so deep, if it be let downe and come to touch it.')

It is remarkable how from the idea of delaying ships the Remora came to be associated with delays in lawsuits and later with delayed births. Elsewhere, Pliny tells that a Remora decided the fate of the Roman Empire in the Battle of Actium, detaining the galley in which Mark Anthony was reviewing his fleet, and that another Remora stopped Caligula's ship despite the efforts of its four hundred oarsmen. 'Let the winds blow as much as they will, rage the stormes and tempests what they can,' exclaims Pliny, 'yet this little fish commandeth their fury, restraineth their puissance, and maugre all their force as great as it is, compelleth ships to stand still: A thing, which no cables, be they neuer so big and strong, no ankers, how massie and weightie soeuer they be, sticke they also as fast and vnmountable as they will, can performe.'

'The mightiest power does not always prevail. A ship may be detained by a small remora,' repeats the fine Spanish writer Diego de Saavedra Fajardo in his *Political Emblems* (1640).

The Rukh

The Rukh (or as it is sometimes given, *roc*) is a vast
magnification of the eagle or vulture, and some people have
thought that a condor blown astray over the Indian Ocean
or China seas suggested it to the Arabs. Lane rejects this idea
and considers that we are dealing rather with a 'fabulous
species of a fabulous genus' or with a synonym for the Persian *Simurgh*. The Rukh is known to the West through the
Arabian Nights. The reader will recall that Sindbad (on his
second voyage), left behind by his shipmates on an island,
found

> a huge white dome rising in air and of vast compass. I
> walked all around it, but found no door thereto, nor could
> I muster strength or nimbleness by reason of its exceeding
> smoothness and slipperiness. So I marked the spot where I
> stood and went round about the dome to measure its cir-
> cumference which I found fifty good paces.

Moments later, a huge cloud hid the sun from him and

> lifting my head ... I saw that the cloud was none other
> than an enormous bird, of gigantic girth and inordinately
> wide of wing ...

The bird was a Rukh and the white dome, of course, was its
egg. Sindbad lashes himself to the bird's leg with his turban,
and the next morning is whisked off into flight and set down
on a mountaintop, without having excited the Rukh's attention. The narrator adds that the Rukh feeds itself on serpents
of such great bulk that they would have made but one gulp
of an elephant.

In Marco Polo's *Travels* (III, 36) we read:

The people of the island [of Madagascar] report that at a certain season of the year, an extraordinary kind of bird which they call a rukh, makes its appearance from the southern region. In form it is said to resemble the eagle but it is incomparably greater in size; being so large and strong as to seize an elephant with its talons, and to lift it into the air, from whence it lets it fall to the ground, in order that when dead it may prey upon the carcase. Persons who have seen this bird assert that when the wings are spread they measure sixteen paces in extent, from point to point; and that the feathers are eight paces in length, and thick in proportion.

Marco Polo adds that some envoys from China brought the feather of a Rukh back to the Grand Khan. A Persian illustration in Lane shows the Rukh bearing off three elephants in beak and talons; 'with the proportion of a hawk and field mice', Burton notes.

The Salamander

Not only is it a small dragon that lives in fire, it is also (according to one dictionary) 'an insectivorous batrachian with intensely black smooth skin and yellow spots'. Of these two characters, the better known is the imaginary, and the Salamander's inclusion in this book will surprise no one.

In Book X of his *Natural History*, Pliny states that the Salamander 'is of so cold a complexion, that if he do but touch the fire, he wil quench it as presently as if ice were put vnto it'; later he thinks this over, observing sceptically that if what magicians said about the Salamander were true, it would be used to put out house fires. In Book XI, he speaks of a four-footed, winged insect – called the 'pyrallis' or 'pyrausta' – living 'in Cypres, among the forges and furnaces of copper . . . [and flying] out of the very midst of the fire'; if it emerges into the air and flies a short distance, it will instantly die. The Salamander in man's memory has incorporated this now forgotten animal.

The phoenix was used as an argument by theologians to prove the resurrection of the flesh; the Salamander, as a proof that bodies can live in fire. In Book XXI of the *City of God* by St Augustine, there is a chapter called *Whether an earthly body may possibly be incorruptible by fire*, and it opens in this way:

> What then shall I say unto the unbelievers, to prove that a body carnal and living may endure undissolved both against death and the force of eternal fire. They will not allow us to ascribe this unto the power of God, but urge us to produce it to them by some example. We shall answer them that there are some creatures that are indeed corruptible, because mortal, and yet do live untouched in the middle of the fire.

Poets, also, flock to the Salamander and phoenix as devices of rhetorical emphasis. Quevedo in the sonnets of the fourth book of his *Spanish Parnassus*, which 'celebrates the exploits of love and beauty', writes:

Hago verdad la Fénix en la ardiente
Llama, en que renaciendo me renuevo;
Y la virilidad del fuego pruebo,
Y que es padre y que tiene descendiente.

La Salamandra fría, que desmiente
Noticia docta, a defender me atrevo,
Cuando en incendios, que sediento bebo,
Mi corazón habita y no los siente.

[I testify to the truth of the Phoenix in burning flames, since I also burn and renew myself, and I prove the maleness of fire, which can be a father and have offspring.

I dare as well defend the cold Salamander, refuted by men

of learning, since my heart dwells in fires, which thirstily
I drink, and feels no pain.]

In the middle of the twelfth century, a forged letter sup-
posedly sent by Prester John, the king of kings, to the Emperor of Byzantium, made its way all over Europe. This
epistle, which is a catalogue of wonders, speaks of gigantic
ants that dig gold, and of a River of Stones, and of a Sea of
Sand with living fish, and of a towering mirror that reflects
whatever happens in the kingdom, and of a sceptre carved
of a single emerald, and of pebbles that make a man invisible
or that light up the night. One of its paragraphs states: 'Our
realm yields the worm known as the salamander. Salamanders live in fire and make cocoons, which our court ladies
spin and use to weave cloth and garments. To wash and
clean these fabrics, they throw them into flames.'

Of these indestructible linens or textiles, which are
cleansed by fire, there is mention in Pliny (XIX, 1) and in
Marco Polo (I, 39). The latter attests that the Salamander is a
substance, not an animal. Nobody, at first, believed him; goods
woven of asbestos and sold as the skins of Salamanders were
an unanswerable proof of the Salamander's existence.

Somewhere in his *Autobiography*, Benvenuto Cellini
writes that at the age of five he saw a tiny animal like a
lizard playing in the fire. He told this to his father, who said
that the animal was a Salamander and gave his son a sound
beating so that the remarkable vision, seldom vouchsafed to
man, would stick forever in the boy's memory.

To the alchemists the Salamander was the spirit of the
element fire. In this symbol and in an argument of
Aristotle's, preserved for us by Cicero in the first book of his
On the Nature of the Gods, we find the reason why men
believed in the Salamander of legend. The Sicilian physician
Empedocles of Agrigentum had formulated the proposition
of the four 'roots', or elements of matter, whose opposition
and affinity, governed by Discord and Love, made up the

cosmic process. There is no death; there are only particles of 'roots', which the Romans were to call 'elements', and which are either falling apart or coming together. These elements are fire, earth, air, and water. They are eternal and none is stronger than any other. Now we know (now we think we know) that this doctrine is false, but men once thought it valuable, and it is generally held that it was on the whole beneficial. Theodor Gomperz has written that 'The four elements which make up and support the world, and which still survive in poetry and in popular imagination, have a long and glorious history.' The system demanded parity: since there were animals of earth and water, animals of fire were needed. For the dignity of science it was essential that Salamanders exist. In a parallel fashion, Aristotle speaks of animals of the air.

Leonardo da Vinci had it that the Salamander fed on fire and in this way renewed its skin.

The Satyrs

Satyrs was the Greek name for them; Rome called them Fauns, Pans, and Sylvans. In the lower part of the body they were goats; their torso, arms, and head were human. Satyrs were thickly covered with hair and had short horns, pointed ears, active eyes, and hooked noses. They were lascivious and fond of their wine. They attended Bacchus in his rollicking and bloodless conquest of India. They set ambushes for nymphs, relished dancing, and their instrument was the flute. Country people paid homage to them, offering them the first fruits of the harvest. Lambs were also sacrificed in their honour.

In Roman times, a specimen of these demigods was surprised asleep in his mountain den in Thessaly by some of

Sulla's soldiers, who brought him before their general. The Satyr uttered inarticulate sounds and was so loathsome to the eyes and nostrils that Sulla had him at once sent back to the wilderness.

A memory of the Satyrs lived on in the medieval image of devils. The word 'satire' seems to have no connection with satyr; most etymologists trace *satire* back to *satura lanx*, a composite dish, hence a mixed literary composition, like the writings of Juvenal.

Scylla

Before becoming a monster and then turned into rocks, Scylla was a nymph with whom Glaucus, one of the sea gods, had fallen in love. In order to win her, Glaucus sought the help of Circe whose knowledge of herbs and incantations was well known. But Circe became attached to Glaucus on sight, only she was unable to get him to forget Scylla, and to punish her rival she poured the juice of poisonous herbs into the fountain where the nymph bathed. At this point, according to Ovid (*Metamorphoses*, XIV, 59–67),

Scylla comes and wades waist-deep into the water; when all at once she sees her loins disfigured with barking monster-shapes. And at the first, not believing that these are parts of her own body, she flees in fear and tries to drive away the boisterous, barking things. But what she flees she takes along with her; and, feeling for her thighs, her legs, her feet, she finds in place of these only gaping dogs'-heads, such as a Cerberus might have. She stands on ravening dogs, and her docked loins and her belly are enclosed in a circle of beastly forms.

She then found herself supported by twelve feet, and she had six heads, each with three rows of teeth. This meta-morphosis so terrified her that she threw herself into the strait separating Italy and Sicily, where the gods changed her into rocks. During storms, sailors speak of the dreadful roaring of the breakers when driven into the uneven cavities of the rock.

This legend is also found in the pages of Homer and Pausanias.

The Sea Horse

Unlike most other imaginary animals, the Sea Horse is not a composite creature; it is no more than a wild horse whose dwelling place is the sea and who comes ashore only on moonless nights when the breezes bring him the smell of mares. On some undetermined island – maybe Borneo – the herders hobble the king's finest mares along the coast and hide themselves underground. Here Sindbad saw the stallion that rose from the sea, watched it leap on to the female, and heard its cry.

The definitive edition of the *Book of a Thousand and One Nights* dates, according to Burton, from the thirteenth century; in this same century lived the cosmographer Zakariyya al-Qaswini who in his treatise *Wonders of Creation* wrote these words: 'The sea horse is like the horse of dry land, but its mane and tail grow longer; its colour is more lustrous and its hooves are cleft like those of wild oxen, while its height is no less than the land horse's and slightly larger than the ass's.' He remarks that a cross between the sea and land species produces a very beautiful breed, and singles out a certain dark pony 'with white spots like pieces of silver'.

An eighteenth-century Chinese traveller, Wang Tai-hai, writes:

The sea horse usually appears along the coast in search of a mare; sometimes he is caught. His coat is black and shining, his tail is long and sweeps the ground. On dry land he goes like any other horse, is very tame, and in a day can travel hundreds of miles. But it is well not to bathe him in the river, for as soon as he sees water he recovers his ancient nature and swims off.

Ethnologists have looked for the origin of this Islamic fiction in the Greco-Roman fiction of the wind that makes mares fertile. In the third book of the *Georgics*, Virgil has set this belief to verse. Pliny's explanation (VIII, 42) is more rigorous:

> In Portugall, along the riuer Tagus, & about Lisbon, certaine it is, that when the west-wind blowes, the mares set vp their tailes, and turne them full against it, and so conceiue that genitall aire in steed of naturall seed: in such sort, as they become great withall, and quicken in their time, & bring forth foles as swift as the wind, but they liue not aboue three yeres.

The hisorian Justinus ventures the guess that the hyperbole 'sons of the wind', applied to very fast horses, gave rise to this fable.

The Shaggy Beast of La Ferté-Bernard

Along the banks of the Huisne, an otherwise peaceful stream, there roamed during the Middle Ages a creature that became known as the Shaggy Beast (*La velue*). This animal had somehow managed to survive the Flood despite its exclusion from the Ark. It was the size of a bull, and it had a snake's head and a round body buried under long green fur. The fur was armed with stingers whose wound was deadly. The creature also had very broad hooves that were similar to the feet of the tortoise, and its tail, shaped like a serpent, could kill men and cattle alike. When its anger was aroused, the Shaggy Beast shot out flames that withered crops. At night it raided stables. Whenever the farmers attempted to hunt it down, it hid in the waters of the Huisne, causing the river to flood its banks and drown the valley for miles.

The Shaggy Beast had a taste for innocent creatures, and devoured maidens and children. It would choose the purest of young womanhood, some Little Lamb (*L'agnelle*). One day, it waylaid one such Little Lamb and dragged her, mauled and bloody, to its lair in the riverbed. The victim's sweetheart tracked the monster, and with a sword sliced into the Shaggy Beast's tail, its only vulnerable spot, and cut it in two. The creature died at once. It was embalmed and its death was celebrated with fifes and drums and dancing.

The Simurgh

The Simurgh is an immortal bird that nests in the branches of the Tree of Knowledge; Burton compares it with the eagle which, according to the Younger Edda, has knowledge of many things and makes its nest in the branches of the World Tree, Yggdrasil.

Both Southey's *Thalaba* (1801) and Flaubert's *Temptation of Saint Anthony* (1874) speak of the Simorg Anka; Flaubert reduces the bird's status to that of an attendant to the Queen of Sheba, and describes it as having orange-coloured feathers like metallic scales, a small silver-coloured head with a human face, four wings, a vulture's talons, and a long, long peacock's tail. In the original sources the Simurgh is a far more important being. Firdausi in the *Book of Kings*, which compiles and sets to verse ancient Iranian legends, makes the bird the foster father of Zal, father of the poem's hero; Farid al-Din Attar, in the twelfth century, makes it a symbol of the godhead. This takes place in the *Mantiq al-Tayr* (Parliament of Birds). The plot of this allegory, made up of some 4,500 couplets, is striking. The distant king of birds, the Simurgh, drops one of his splendid feathers somewhere in the middle of China; on learning of this, the other birds, tired of their present anarchy, decide to seek him. They know that the king's name means 'thirty birds'; they know that his castle lies in the Kaf, the mountain or range of mountains that ring the earth. At the outset, some of the birds lose heart: the nightingale pleads his love for the rose; the parrot pleads his beauty, for which he lives caged; the partridge cannot do without his home in the hills, nor the heron without his marsh, nor the owl without his ruins. But finally, certain of them set out on the perilous venture; they cross seven valleys or seas, the next to last bearing the name Bewilderment, the last the name Annihilation. Many of the pilgrims desert; the journey takes its toll among the rest. Thirty, made pure by their sufferings, reach the great peak of the Simurgh. At last they behold him; they realize that they are the Simurgh, and that the Simurgh is each of them and all of them.

Edward FitzGerald translated portions of the poem under the playful title *The Bird-Parliament; A bird's-eye view of Faríd-Uddín Attar's Bird-Parliament.*

The cosmographer al-Qaswini, in his *Wonders of Creation*, states that the Simorg Anka lives for seventeen hundred years and that, upon the coming of age of its son, the father burns himself on a funeral pyre. 'This,' observes Lane, 'reminds us of the phoenix.'

Sirens

Through the course of time the image of the Sirens has changed. Their first historian, Homer, in the twelfth book of the *Odyssey*, does not tell us what they were like; to Ovid, they are birds of reddish plumage with the faces of young girls; to Apollonius of Rhodes, in the upper part of the body they are women and in the lower part seabirds; to the Spanish playwright Tirso de Molina (and to heraldry), 'half woman, half fish'. No less debatable is their nature. In his classical dictionary Lemprière calls them nymphs; in Quicherat's they are monsters, and in Grimal's they are demons. They inhabit a western island, close to Circe's, but the dead body of one of them, Parthenope, was found washed ashore in Campania and gave her name to the famed city now called Naples. Strabo, the geographer, saw her grave and witnessed the games held periodically in her memory.

The *Odyssey* tells that the Sirens attract and shipwreck seamen, and that Ulysses, in order to hear their song and yet remain alive, plugged the ears of his oarsmen with wax and had himself lashed to the mast. The Sirens, tempting him, promised him knowledge of all the things of this world:

> For never yet has any man rowed past this isle in his black ship until he has heard the sweet voice from our lips. Nay, he has joy of it, and goes his way a wiser man. For we know all the toils that in wide Troy the Argives and Trojans endured through the will of the gods, and we know all things that come to pass upon the fruitful earth.

A legend recorded by the mythologist Apollodorus in his *Bibliotheca*, tells that Orpheus, aboard the Argonauts' ship, sang more sweetly than the Sirens and that because of this these creatures threw themselves into the sea and were changed into rocks, for their fate was to die whenever their spell went unheeded. The sphinx, also, threw herself from a precipice when her riddle was solved.

In the sixth century, a Siren was caught and baptized in northern Wales, and in certain old calendars took her place as a saint under the name Murgen. Another, in 1403, slipped through a breach in a dike and lived in Haarlem until the day of her death. Nobody could make out her speech, but she was taught to weave and she worshipped the cross as if instinctively. A chronicler of the sixteenth century argued that she was not a fish because she knew how to weave and that she was not a woman because she was able to live in water.

The English language distinguishes between the classical Siren and the mermaid, which has the tail of a fish. The making of this later image may have been influenced by the Tritons, who were lesser divinities in the court of Poseidon.

In the tenth book of Plato's *Republic*, eight Sirens rule over the revolution of the eight concentric heavens.

Siren: a suppposed marine animal, we read in a brutally frank dictionary.

The Sow Harnessed with Chains and other Argentine Fauna

On page 106 of his *Dictionary of Argentine Folklore*, Felix Coluccio records:

In the northern part of Córdoba, especially around Quilinos, people speak of a sow harnessed with chains which commonly makes its presence known in the hours of night. Those living close to the railroad station maintain that the sow slides on the tracks, and others assured us that it is not unusual for the sow to run along the telegraph wires, producing a deafening racket with its 'chains'. As yet, nobody has caught a glimpse of the animal, for as soon as you look for it, it vanishes unaccountably.

Belief in the Sow Harnessed with Chains (*chancha con cadenas*), which also goes by the name of the Tin Pig (*chancho de lata*), is prevalent as well in the Province of Buenos Aires in slums and towns along the riverside.

There are two Argentine versions of the werewolf. One of them, common also to Uruguay and to southern Brazil, is the *lobisón*; but since no wolves inhabit these regions, men are supposed to take the shapes of swine or dogs. In certain towns of Entre Ríos, girls shun young men who live in the vicinity of stockyards because on Saturday nights they are said to turn into the aforementioned animals. In the midland provinces, we find the *tigre capiango*. This beast is not a jaguar but a man who, at will, can take the jaguar's form. Usually his purpose is to frighten friends in a spirit of rustic jesting, but highwaymen have also availed themselves of the guise. During the civil wars of the last century, General Facundo Quiroga was popularly supposed to have under his command an entire regiment of *capiangos*.

The Sphinx

The Sphinx of Egyptian monuments (called by Herodotus *androsphinx*, or man-sphinx, in order to distinguish it from the Greek Sphinx) is a lion having the head of a man and lying at rest; it stood watch by temples and tombs, and is said to have represented royal authority. In the halls of Karnak, other Sphinxes have the head of a ram, the sacred animal of Amon. The Sphinx of Assyrian monuments is a winged bull with a man's bearded and crowned head; this image is common on Persian gems. Pliny in his list of Ethiopian animals includes the Sphinx; of them, he says only that they are common, 'with a browne duskish haire, [and] hauing dugs in their brest'.

The Greek Sphinx has a woman's head and breasts, the wings of a bird, and the body and feet of a lion. Some give it the body of a dog and a snake's tail. It is told that it depopulated the Theban countryside asking riddles (for it had a human voice) and making a meal of any man who could not give the answer. Of Oedipus, the son of Jocasta, the Sphinx asked, 'What has four legs, two legs, and three legs, and the more legs it has the weaker it is?' (So runs what seems to be the oldest version. In time the metaphor was introduced which makes of man's life a single day. Nowadays the question goes, Which animal walks on four legs in the morning, two legs at noon, and three in the evening?') Oedipus answered that it was a man who as an infant crawls on all fours, when he grows up walks on two legs, and in old age leans on a staff. The riddle solved, the Sphinx threw herself from a precipice.

De Quincey, around 1849, suggested a second interpretation, which complements the traditional one. The subject of the riddle according to him is not so much man in general as it is Oedipus in particular, orphaned and helpless at birth, alone in his manhood, and supported by Antigone in his blind and hopeless old age.

The Squonk

(*Lacrimacorpus dissolvens*)

The range of the squonk is very limited. Few people outside of Pennsylvania have ever heard of the quaint beast, which is said to be fairly common in the hemlock forests of that State. The squonk is of a very retiring disposition, generally travelling about at twilight and dusk. Because of its misfitting skin, which is covered with warts and moles, it is always unhappy; in fact it is said, by people who are best able to judge, to be the most morbid of beasts. Hunters who are good at tracking are able to follow a squonk by its tear-stained trail, for the animal weeps constantly. When cornered and escape seems impossible, or when surprised and frightened, it may even dissolve itself in tears. Squonk hunters are most successful on frosty moonlight nights, when tears are shed slowly and the animal dislikes moving about; it may then be heard weeping under the boughs of dark hemlock trees. Mr J. P. Wentling, formerly of Pennsylvania, but now at St Anthony Park, Minnesota, had a disappointing experience with a squonk near Mont Alto. He made a clever capture by mimicking the squonk and inducing it to hop into a sack, in which he was carrying it home, when suddenly the burden lightened and the weeping ceased. Wentling unslung the sack and looked in. There was nothing but tears and bubbles.

WILLIAM T. COX:
Fearsome Creatures of the Lumberwoods,
With a Few Desert and Mountain Beasts

Swedenborg's Angels

For the last twenty-five years of his studious life, the eminent philosopher and man of science Emanuel Swedenborg (1688–1772) resided in London. But as the English are not very talkative, he fell into the habit of conversing with devils and Angels. God granted him the privilege of visiting the Other World and of entering into the lives of its inhabitants. Christ had said that souls, in order to be admitted into Heaven, must be righteous. Swedenborg added that they must also be intelligent; later on Blake stipulated that they should be artists and poets. Swedenborg's Angels are those souls who have chosen Heaven. They need no words; it is enough that an Angel only think of another in order to have him at his side. Two people who have loved each other on earth become a single Angel. Their world is ruled by love; every Angel is a Heaven. Their shape is that of a perfect human being; Heaven's shape is the same. The Angels, in whatever direction they look – north, east, south, or west – are always face to face with God. They are, above all, divines; their chief delight lies in prayer and in the unravelling of theological problems. Earthly things are but emblems of heavenly things. The sun stands for the godhead. In Heaven there is no time; the appearance of things changes according to moods. The Angels' garments shine according to their intelligence. The souls of the rich are richer than the souls of the poor, since the rich are accustomed to wealth. In Heaven, all objects, furniture, and cities are more physical and more complex than those of our earth; colours are more varied and splendid. Angels of English stock show a tendency to politics; Jews to the sale of trinkets; Germans tote bulky volumes which they consult before venturing an answer. Since Moslems venerate Mohammed, God has provided them with an Angel who impersonates the Prophet. The poor in spirit and hermits are denied the pleasures of Heaven, for they would be unable to enjoy them.

Swedenborg's Devils

In the works of the famous eighteenth-century Swedish visionary, we read that Devils, like angels, are not a species apart but derive from the human race. They are individuals who after death choose Hell. There, in that region of marshlands, of desert wastes, of tangled forests, of towns levelled by fire, of brothels, and of gloomy dens, they feel no special happiness, but in Heaven they would be far unhappier still. Occasionally, a ray of heavenly light falls on them from on high; the Devils feel it as a burning, a scorching, and it reaches their nostrils as a stench. Each thinks himself handsome, but many have the faces of beasts or have shapeless lumps of flesh where faces should be; others are faceless. They live in a state of mutual hatred and of armed violence, and if they come together it is for the purpose of plotting against one another or of destroying each other. God has forbidden men and angels to draw a map of Hell, but we know that its general outline follows that of a Devil, just as the outline of Heaven follows that of an angel. The most vile and loathsome Hells lie to the west.

The Sylphs

To each of the four roots, or elements, into which the Greeks divided all matter, a particular spirit was later made to correspond. Paracelsus, the sixteenth-century Swiss alchemist and physician, gave them their names: the Gnomes of earth, the Nymphs of water, the Salamanders of fire, and the Sylphs, or Sylphides, of air. All of these words come from the Greek. The French philologist Littré traced the etymology of 'sylph' to the Celtic languages, but it seems quite unlikely that Paracelsus, who gave us the name, knew anything about those tongues.

No one any longer believes in the Sylphs, but the word is used as a trivial compliment applied to a slender young woman. Sylphs occupy an intermediate place between supernatural and natural beings; Romantic poets and the ballet have not neglected them.

Talos

Living beings made of metal or stone make up some of fantastic zoology's most alarming species. Let us recall the angry bulls with brass feet and horns that breathed flames and that Jason, helped by the magic arts of Medea, yoked to the plough; Condillac's psychological statue of sensitive marble; the boatman in the *Arabian Nights*, 'a man of brass with a tablet of lead on his breast inscribed with talismans and characts', who rescued the third Kalandar from the Magnet Mountain; the 'girls of mild silver, or of furious gold', which a goddess in William Blake's mythology caught in silken nets for the delight of her lover; and the metal birds who nursed Ares.

To this list we may also add a draft animal, the swift wild boar Gullinbursti, whose name means 'golden-bristled'. The mythologist Paul Herrmann writes: 'This living piece of metalwork came from the forge of skilful dwarfs; they threw a pigskin into the fire and drew out a golden boar with the power of travelling on land, sea, and air. However dark the night, there is always light enough in the boar's path.' Gullinbursti pulled the chariot of Freya, the Norse goddess of love, marriage, and fertility.

And then there is Talos, the warden of the island of Crete. Some consider this giant the work of Vulcan or of Daedalus; Apollonius of Rhodes tells us about him in his *Argonautica* (IV, 1638–48):

> And Talos, the man of bronze, as he broke off the rocks from the hard cliff, stayed them from fastening hawsers to the shore, when they came to the roadstead of Dicte's haven. He was of the stock of bronze, of the men sprung from ash-trees, the last left among the sons of the gods; and the son of Cronos gave him to Europa to be the warder of Crete and to stride round the island thrice a day with his feet of bronze. Now in all the rest of his body and limbs was he fashioned of bronze and invulnerable; but beneath the sinew by his ankle was a blood-red vein; and this, with its issues of life and death, was covered by a thin skin.

It was through this vulnerable heel, of course, that Talos met his end. Medea bewitched him with a hostile glance, and when the giant again began heaving boulders from his cliff, 'he grazed his ankle on a pointed crag, and the ichor gushed forth like melted lead; and not long thereafter did he stand towering on the jutting cliff'.

In another version of the myth, Talos, burning red-hot,

would put his arms around a man and kill him. The bronze giant this time met death at the hands of Castor and Pollux, the Dioscuri, who were led on by the sorceress Medea.

The T'ao T'ieh

Poets and mythology seem to have ignored it, but everyone at some time has discovered a T'ao T'ieh for himself at the corner of a capital or in the middle of a frieze, and felt a slight uneasiness. The dog that guarded the flocks of the threefold Geryon had two heads and a single body, and luckily was killed by Hercules. The T'ao T'ieh inverts this order and is still more horrible: its huge head is connected to one body on the right and another on the left. Generally it has six legs since the front pair serves for both bodies. Its face may be a dragon's, a tiger's, or a person's; art historians call it an 'ogre's mask'. It is a formal monster, inspired by the demon of symmetry for sculptors, potters, and ceramicists. Some fourteen hundred years B.C., under the Shang Dynasty, it already figured on ceremonial bronzes.

T'ao T'ieh means 'glutton' and it embodies the vices of sensuality and avarice. The Chinese paint it on their dishes in order to warn against self-indulgence.

Thermal Beings

It was revealed to the visionary and theosophist Rudolf Steiner (1861–1925) that this planet, before it was the earth we now know, passed through a solar stage, and before that through a Saturnian stage. Man today is composed of a physical body, of an ethereal body, of an astral body, and of an ego; at the start of the Saturnian period he was a physical body only. This body was neither visible nor tangible, since at that time there were on earth neither solids nor liquids nor gases. There were only states of heat, thermal forms, defining in cosmic space regular and irregular figures; each man, each being, was an organism made of changing temperatures. According to the testimony of Steiner, mankind during the Saturnian period was a blind, deaf, and insensitive multitude of articulated states of heat and cold. 'To the investigator, heat is but a substance still subtler than a gas,' we read in one page of Steiner's *Die Geheimwissenschaft im Umriss* (Outline of Occult Science). Before the solar stage, fire spirits, or archangels, animated the bodies of those 'men', who began to glow and shine.

Did Steiner dream these things? Did he dream them because they had occurred ages earlier? What is undeniable is that they are far stranger than the demiurges, serpents, and bulls of other cosmogonies.

The Tigers of Annam

To the Annamites, tigers, or spirits who dwell in tigers, govern the four corners of space. The Red Tiger rules over the South (which is located at the top of maps); summer and fire belong to him. The Black Tiger rules over the North; winter and water belong to him. The Blue Tiger rules over the East; spring and plants belong to him. The White Tiger rules over the West; autumn and metals belong to him.

Over these Cardinal Tigers is a fifth tiger, the Yellow Tiger, who stands in the middle governing the others, just as the Emperor stands in the middle of China and China in the middle of the World. (That's why it is called the Middle Kingdom; that's why it occupies the middle of the map that Father Ricci, of the Society of Jesus, drew at the end of the sixteenth century for the instruction of the Chinese.)

Lao-tzu entrusted to the Five Tigers the mission of waging war against devils. An Annamite prayer, translated into French by Louis Cho Chod, implores the aid of the Five Heavenly Tigers. This superstition is of Chinese origin; Sinologists speak of a White Tiger that rules over the remote region of the western stars. To the South the Chinese place a Red Bird; to the East, a Blue Dragon; to the North, a Black Tortoise. As we see, the Annamites have preserved the colours but have made the animals one.

The Bhils, a people of Central India, believe in hells for Tigers; the Malays tell of a city in the heart of the jungle with beams of human bones, walls of human skin, and eaves of human hair, built and inhabited by Tigers.

The Trolls

In England, after the advent of Christianity, the Valkyries (or 'Choosers of the Slain') were relegated to the villages and there degenerated into witches; in the Scandinavian countries the giants of heathen myth, who lived in Jotunnheim and battled against the god Thor, were reduced to rustic Trolls. In the cosmogony opening the Elder Edda, we read that in the Twilight of the Gods, the giants, allied with a wolf and a serpent, wil scale the rainbow Bifrost, which will break under their weight, thereby destroying the world. The Trolls of popular superstition are stupid, evil elves who dwell in mountain crannies or in ramshackle huts. Trolls of distinction may bear two or three heads.

Henrik Ibsen's dramatic poem *Peer Gynt* (1867) assures them their immortality. Ibsen depicts the Trolls as, above all, nationalists. They think, or do their best to think, that the foul concoction they brew is delicious and that their hovels are palaces. So that Peer Gynt would not witness the sordidness of his surroundings and the ugliness of the princess he is about to marry, the Trolls offer to put out his eyes.

Two Metaphysical Beings

The mystery of the origin of ideas brings a pair of strange creatures to imaginary zoology. One was evolved towards the middle of the eighteenth century, the other a hundred years later.

The first is Condillac's sensitive statue. Descartes professed the Platonic doctrine of innate ideas; Étienne Bonnot de Condillac, for the purposes of refuting him, conceived a marble statue in the likeness of the human body and inhabited by a soul that had never perceived or thought. Condillac begins by conferring on his statue a single sense, perhaps the least complex of all – that of smell. A whiff of jasmine is the start of the statue's biography; for one moment there is nothing but this odour in the whole universe – or, to be more accurate, this odour is the universe, which a moment later will be the odour of a rose, then of a carnation. In the statue's consciousness, once there is a single odour we have attention; once an odour lasts after the stimulus has ceased we have memory; once a present and a past impression occupy the statue's attention we have the ability to compare; once the statue perceives likeness and unlikeness we have judgement; once the ability to compare and judgement occur a second time we have reflection; once a pleasant memory is more vivid than an unpleasant impression we have imagination. Once the faculty of understanding is born, the faculty of the will will be born: love and hate (attraction and repulsion), hope and fear. The consciousness of having passed through many states of mind will give the statue the abstract notion of numbers; the consciousness of being the odour of carnation and of having been the odour of jasmine, the notion of the I.

The author will then endow his hypothetical man with hearing, taste, sight, and finally, touch. This last sense will reveal to him that space exists and that in space he exists in a body; sounds, smells, and colours had been to him, before this stage, mere variations or modifications of his consciousness.

The allegory just related is called *Traité des sensations* and dates from 1754; for this summary we have made use of the second volume of Bréhier's *Histoire de la philosophie*.

The other creature raised by the problem of consciousness is the 'hypothetical animal' of Rudolf Hermann Lotze. Lonelier than the statue that smells roses and finally becomes a man, this being has in its skin but one movable sensitive point – at the extremity of an antenna. Its structure denies it, as is obvious, more than one perception at a time. Lotze argues that the ability to retract or extend its sensitive antenna will enable this all but bereft animal to discover the external world (without the aid of the Kantian categories of time and space) and distinguish a stationary from a moving object. This fiction may be found in the book *Medizinische Psychologie* (1852); it has been praised by Hans Vaihinger.

The Unicorn

The first version of the Unicorn is nearly identical with the latest. Four hundred years B.C., the Greek historian and physician Ctesias told that among the kingdoms of India there were very swift wild asses with white coats, purple heads, blue eyes, and in the middle of their foreheads a pointed horn whose base was white, whose tip was red, and whose middle was black. Pliny, more precise, wrote (VIII, 21):

> the most fell and furious beast of all other is the Licorne or Monoceros: his body resembles a horse, his head a stag, his feet an Elephant, his taile a bore; he loweth after an hideous manner, one black horne he hath in the mids of his forehead, bearing out two cubits in length: by report, this wild beast cannot possibly be caught aliue.

Around 1892, the Orientalist Schrader conjectured that the Unicorn might have been suggested to the Greeks by certain Persian bas-reliefs depicting bulls in profile with a single horn.

In Isidore of Seville's *Etymologies*, composed at the beginning of the seventh century, we read that one thrust of the Unicorn's horn may kill an elephant; this perhaps is echoed in the similar victory, in Sindbad's second voyage, of the Karkadan, or rhinoceros, which can 'carry off a great elephant on its horn'. (We also find here that the rhinoceros's horn 'cleft in twain, is the likeness of a man'; al-Qaswini says it is the likeness of a man on horseback, and others have spoken of birds and fishes.) Another of the Unicorn's enemies was the lion, and a stanza in the tangled allegory *The Faerie Queene* records the manner of their duel in this way:

Like as a Lyon, whose imperiall powre
A prowd rebellious Unicorn defyes,
T' avoide the rash assault and wrathful stowre
Of his fiers foe, him to a tree applyes,
And when him ronning in full course he spyes,
He slips aside; the whiles that furious beast
His precious horne, sought of his enimyes,
Strikes in the stocke, ne thence can be releast,
But to the mighty victor yields a bounteous feast.

These lines (Book II, Canto V, Stanza X) date from the six-teenth century; at the beginning of the eighteenth century, the union of the Kingdom of England with the Kingdom of Scotland brought together on the heraldic arms of Great Britain the English Leopard, or Lion, and the Scottish Uni-corn.

In the Middle Ages, bestiaries taught that the Unicorn could be captured by a maiden; in the Greek *Physiologus* we read: 'How it is captured. A virgin is placed before it and it springs into the virgin's lap and she warms it with love and carries it off to the palace of kings.' One of Pisanello's medals and many famous tapestries illustrate this victory whose allegorical applications are obvious. Leonardo da Vinci attributes the Unicorn's capture to its lust, which makes it forget its fierceness, lie in a girl's lap, and so be taken by hunters. The Holy Ghost, Jesus Christ, mercury, and evil have all been represented by the Unicorn. In his *Psychologie und Alchemie* (1944), Jung gives a history and an analysis of these symbols.

A small white horse with the forelegs of an antelope, a goat's beard, and a long twisted horn projecting straight out from its forehead is the picture usually given of this imagin-ary animal.

The Unicorn of China

The Chinese Unicorn, the *k'i-lin*, is one of the four animals of good omen; the others are the dragon, the phoenix, and the tortoise. The Unicorn is foremost of all the 360 creatures that live on land. It has the body of a deer, the tail of an ox, and the hooves of a horse. Its short horn, which grows out of its forehead, is made of flesh; its coat, on its back, is of five mixed colours, while its belly is brown or yellow. It is so gentle that when it walks it is careful not to tread on the tiniest living creature and will not even eat live grass but only what is dead. Its appearance foretells the birth of an upright ruler. To wound the Chinese Unicorn or to come across its dead body is unlucky. The span of this animal's natural life is a thousand years.

When Confucius' mother bore him in her womb, the spirits of the five planets brought her an animal 'having the shape of a cow, scales of a dragon, and a horn on its forehead'. This is the way Soothill reports the annunciation; a variant of this given by Wilhelm tells that the animal appeared on its own and spat out a jade tablet on which these words were read:

> Son of mountain crystal [or of the essence of water], when the dynasty crumbles, thou shalt rule as a throneless king.

Seventy years later, some hunters killed a *k'i-lin* which still had a bit of ribbon around its horn that Confucius' mother had tied there. Confucius went to look at the Unicorn and wept because he felt what the death of this innocent and mysterious animal foretold, and because in that ribbon lay his past.

In the thirteenth century, a scouting expedition of the

Emperor Genghis Khan, who had undertaken the invasion of India, met a creature in the desert 'like a deer, with a head like that of a horse, one horn on its forehead, and green hair on its body', which addressed them, saying, 'It is time for your master to return to his own land.' One of Genghis' Chinese ministers, upon consultation, explained to him that the animal was a *chio-tuan*, a variety of the k'ilin. 'For four years the great army has been warring in western regions,' he said. 'Heaven, which has a horror of bloodshed, gives warning through the *Chio-tuan*. Spare the Empire for Heaven's sake; moderation will give boundless pleasure.' The Emperor desisted in his war plans.

Twenty-two centuries before the Christian era, one of the judges of the Emperor Shun was in possession of a 'one-horned goat' which refused to attack the wrongly accused but would butt the guilty.

Margoulies' *Anthologie raisonnée de la littérature chinoise* (1948) includes this mysterious, soft-spoken allegory, the work of a ninth-century writer of prose:

> It is universally held that the unicorn is a supernatural being and of auspicious omen; so say the odes, the annals, the biographies of worthies, and other texts whose authority is unimpeachable. Even village women and children know that the unicorn is a lucky sign. But this animal does not figure among the barnyard animals, it is not always easy to come across, it does not lend itself to zoological classification. Nor is it like the horse or bull, the wolf or deer. In such circumstances we may be face to face with a unicorn and not know for sure that we are. We know that a certain animal with a mane is a horse and that a certain animal with horns is a bull. We do not know what the unicorn looks like.

The Uroboros

To us the ocean is a sea or a system of seas; to the Greeks it was a simple circular river that ringed the land mass. All streams flowed from it and it had neither outlets nor sources. It was also a god or a Titan, perhaps the most ancient of all Titans, since Sleep in Book XIV of the *Iliad* calls it the source from whom the gods are sprung. In Hesiod's *Theogony*, it is the father of all the world's rivers – three thousand in number – the leading of which are the Alpheus and the Nile. An old man with a flowing beard was the usual personification of the river-ocean; after centuries men found a better symbol.

Heraclitus had said that in the circumference the beginning and the end are a single point. A third-century Greek amulet, preserved in the British Museum, gives us the image which best illustrates this endlessness: the serpent that bites its own tail or, as the Argentine poet Martínez Estrada so beautifully put it, 'that begins at the end of its tail'. A story runs that Mary Queen of Scots had engraved on a gold ring the inscription 'In my end is my beginning,' meaning perhaps that real life begins after death. Uroboros (Greek for 'the one that devours its tail') is the learned name of this creature which became the symbol adopted by alchemists in the Middle Ages. The curious may read further in Jung's study *Psychologie und Alchemie*.

A world-circling serpent is also found in Norse cosmology; it is called the Miðgarðsormr – literally, the middle-yard's-worm, middle-yard standing for the earth. In the Younger Edda, Snorri Sturluson recorded that Loki fathered a wolf and a serpent. An oracle warned the gods that these creatures would be the earth's downfall. The wolf, Fenrir, was kept on a cord woven of six imaginary things: 'the noise of a cat's footfall, the beards of women, the roots of stones, the sinews of bears, the breath of fish, and the spittle of birds.' The serpent, Jormungard, 'was thrown into the sea surrounding the land and there it has grown so large that now it too surrounds the earth and bites its own tail.'

In Jotunnheim, the land of giants, Utgard-Loki challenges the god Thor to pick up a cat; Thor, using all his strength, barely manages to lift one of the cat's paws off the ground. The cat is really the serpent. Thor has been tricked by magic.

At the Twilight of the Gods the serpent will devour the earth and the wolf the sun.

The Valkyries

Valkyrie means, in early German languages, the 'chooser of the slain'. We do not know how the people of Germany and of Austria imagined them; in Norse mythology they are lovely maidens who bear weapons. Their usual number was three, though in the Eddas the names of more than a dozen are given.

In popular myth they took the souls of those slain in battle and brought them to Odin's epic paradise. There, in the Hall of the Slain, Valhalla, whose ceiling was of gold and was lighted by drawn swords and not lamps, the warriors battled from daybreak to sunset. Then those of them who had been killed were brought back to life, and all shared a divine feast in which they were served the meat of an immortal wild boar and inexhaustible hornfuls of mead. This idea of an endless battle seems to be Celtic in origin.

An Anglo-Saxon charm against the pain of sudden stitches

describes the Valkyries without naming them; the lines, as translated by Stopford A. Brooke, run this way:

Loud were they, lo! loud, as over the land they rode;
Fierce of heart were they, as over the hill they rode!

. . . . . .

For the mighty maidens have mustered up their strength . . .

Under the spreading influence of Christianity, the name Valkyrie degenerated; in medieval England a judge had burned at the stake an unlucky woman charged with being a Valkyrie, that is to say, a witch.

The Western Dragon

A tall-standing, heavy serpent with claws and wings is perhaps the description that best fits the Dragon. It may be black, but it is essential that it also be shining; equally essential is that it belch forth fire and smoke. The above description refers, of course, to its present image; the Greeks seem to have applied the name Dragon to any considerable reptile. Pliny informs us that in summer the Dragon craves elephant blood, which is notably cool. It will make a sudden foray on the elephant, coil round it, and plunge its teeth into it. The bloodless elephant rolls on the ground and dies; so does the Dragon, crushed under the weight of its victim. We also read that Ethiopian Dragons, in search of better pasturage, regularly cross the Red Sea and migrate to Arabia. To accomplish this, four or five Dragons coil together and form a kind of craft, with their heads lifted out of the water. In Pliny there is also a chapter devoted to remedies derived from the Dragon. Here we read that its eyes, dried and then stirred with honey, make a liniment that is effective against nightmares. The fat of the Dragon's heart stored in the hide of a gazelle and tied to the arm with the sinews of a stag assures success in litigation; Dragon teeth, also bound to the body, ensure the indulgence of masters and the mercy of kings. With some scepticism Pliny cites a preparation that renders men invincible. It is concocted of the skin of a lion, a lion's marrow, the froth of a horse which has just won a race, the nails of a dog, and the tail and head of a Dragon.

In the eleventh book of the *Iliad* we read that there was a blue three-headed Dragon on Agamemnon's shield; centuries later Norse pirates painted Dragons on their shields and carved Dragon heads on the prows of their long ships. Among the Romans, the Dragon was the insignia of the cohort, as the eagle was of the legion; this is the origin of present-day dragoons. On the standards of the Saxon kings of England there were Dragons; the object of such images was to impart fear to enemy ranks. In the ballad of Athis, we read:

Ce souloient Romains porter,
Ce nous fait moult à redouter.

[This was what the Romans used to bear, this which makes us so feared.]

In the West, the Dragon was always thought of as evil. One of the stock exploits of heroes (Hercules, Sigurd, St Michael, St George) was to overcome and slay a Dragon. In Germanic myth, the Dragon kept watch over precious objects. And so in *Beowulf*, written in England in the seventh or eighth century, there is a Dragon that stands guard over a treasure for some three hundred years. A runaway slave hides in its lair and steals a cup. On waking, the Dragon notices the theft and resolves to kill the thief, but every once in a while goes back inside to make sure the cup has not been merely mislaid. (How strange of the poet to attribute to his monster so human a misgiving.) The Dragon begins to ravage the kingdom; Beowulf searches it out, grapples with it, and kills it, dying himself soon after from a mortal wound inflicted by the Dragon's tusks.

People believed in the reality of the Dragon. In the middle of the sixteenth century, the Dragon is recorded in Conrad Gesner's *Historia Animalium*, a work of a scientific nature.

Time has notably worn away the Dragon's prestige. We believe in the lion as reality and symbol; we believe in the Minotaur as symbol but no longer as reality. The Dragon is perhaps the best known but also the least fortunate of fantastic animals. It seems childish to us and usually spoils the stories in which it appears. It is worth remembering, however, that we are dealing with a modern prejudice, due perhaps to a surfeit of Dragons in fairy tales. In the Revelations, St John speaks twice of the Dragon, 'that old serpent, called the Devil and Satan . . .' In the same spirit, St Augustine writes that the Devil 'is lion and dragon; lion for its rage, dragon for its cunning'. Jung observes that in the Dragon are the reptile and the bird – the elements of earth and of air.

Youwarkee

In his *Short History of English Literature*, Saintsbury finds the flying girl Youwarkee one of the most charming heroines of the eighteenth-century novel. Half woman and half bird, or – as Browning was to write of his dead wife, Elizabeth Barrett – half angel and half bird, she can open her arms and make wings of them, and a silky down covers her body. She lives on an island lost in Antarctic seas and was discovered there by Peter Wilkins, a shipwrecked sailor, who marries her. Youwarkee is a *gawry* (or flying woman) and belongs to a race of flying people known as *glumms*. Wilkins converts them to Christianity and, after the death of his wife, succeeds in making his way back to England.

The story of this strange love affair may be read in the novel *Peter Wilkins* (1751) by Robert Paltock.

The Zaratan

There is one story that has ranged the whole of geography and all epochs – the tale of mariners who land on an unknown island which then sinks into the sea and drowns them because it is a living creature. This invention is found in the first voyage of Sindbad and in Canto VI, Stanza 37, of *Orlando Furioso* (*Ch'ella sia una isoletta ci credemo* – 'We believed it [the whale] to be a small island'); in the Irish legend of St Brendan and in the Greek bestiary of Alexandria; in the *Historia de Gentibus Septentrionalibus* (Rome, 1555) by the Swedish ecclesiastic Olaus Magnus and in this passage from the opening of *Paradise Lost*, in which Satan, 'stretched out huge in length', is compared to a whale (203–8):

> Him haply slumbering on the Norway foam,
> The pilot of some small night-foundered skiff
> Deeming some island, oft, as seamen tell,
> With fixed anchor in his scaly rind,
> Moors by his side under the lee, while night
> Invests the sea . . .

Paradoxically, one of the earliest versions of the legend gives it in order to refute it. This is recorded in the *Book of*

Animals by al-Jahiz, the ninth-century Moslem zoologist. We translate its words from the Spanish version by Miguel Asín Palacios:

As for the zaratan, I never met anyone who actually saw it with his own eyes.

There are sailors who assert that they have drawn alongside certain sea islands, seeing wooded valleys and crevices in the rock, and landed to light a big fire; and when the heat of the flames reached the zaratan's spine, the beast began to slip under the waters with them on top of him, and with all the plants growing on him, until only those able to swim away were saved. This outdoes even the boldest, most imaginative piece of fiction.

Let us now consider a thirteenth-century text by al-Qaswini, the Persian cosmographer who wrote in Arabic. It comes from a work of his entitled *Wonders of Creation*, and runs this way:

As for the sea turtle, it is of such huge size that people on shipboard take it for an island. One merchant has reported:

'Rising out of the sea we discovered an island with green plants, and we went ashore and dug pits for a cooking fire, and the island began to move and the sailors said: "Back to the ship! It's a turtle! The heat of the fires has wakened him and we'll be lost!"'

This story is repeated in the *Navigation of St Brendan:*

And than they sayled forth, and came soone after to that lond; but bycause of the lytell depthe in some place, and in some place were grete rockes, but at the last they wente upon an ylonde, wenynge to them they had ben safe, and made theron a fyre for to dresse theyr dyner, but saynt Brandon abode styll in the shyppe. And whan the fyre was ryght hote, and the meet nygh soden, than this ylonde began to move; whereof the monkes were aferde, and fledde anone to the shyppe, and lefte the fyre and meet behynde them, and mervayled sore of the movying. And saynt Brandon comforted them, and sayd that it was a grete fisshe named Jasconye, whiche laboureth nyght and daye to put his tayle in his mouth, but for gretnes he may not.

In the Anglo-Saxon bestiary of the *Exeter Book*, the dangerous island is a whale, 'skilled in treachery', that deliberately tricks seafarers. They camp on its back seeking rest from their labours at sea; suddenly the Ocean's Guest sinks down and the men drown. In the Greek bestiary, the whale stands for the whore of the Proverbs ('Her feet go down to death, her steps take hold on hell'); in the Anglo-Saxon bestiary it stands for the Devil and Evil. These same symbolic values will be found in *Moby Dick*, written ten centuries later.

Index

164

More About Penguins
and Pelicans

Penguinews, which appears every month, contains details of all the new books issued by Penguins as they are published. It is supplemented by our stocklist, which includes almost 5,000 titles.

A specimen copy of *Penguinews* will be sent to you free on request. Please write to Dept EP, Penguin Books Ltd, Harmondsworth, Middlesex, for your copy.

In the U.S.A.: For a complete list of books available from Penguins in the United States write to Dept CS, Penguin Books, 625 Madison Avenue, New York, New York 10022.

In Canada: For a complete list of books available from Penguins in Canada write to Penguin Books Canada Ltd, 2801 John Street, Markham, Ontario L3R 1B4.

In Australia: For a complete list of books available from Penguins in Australia write to the Marketing Department, Penguin Books Australia Ltd, P.O. Box 257, Ringwood, Victoria 3134.

Jorge Luis Borges

'A great writer who has composed only little essays or
short narratives. Yet they suffice for us to call him great
because of their wonderful intelligence, their wealth of
invention and their tight, almost mathematical, style' –
André Maurois in his introduction to *Labyrinths*

Doctor Brodie's Report

In the preface Borges writes: 'I have done my best – I
don't know with what success – to write straightforward
stories. I do not dare to state that they are simple; there
isn't anywhere on earth a single page or single word that
is, since each thing implies the universe, whose most
obvious trait is complexity ... My stories, like those of
the *Thousand and One Nights,* try to be entertaining or
moving but not persuasive ... The art of writing is
mysterious; the opinions we hold ephemeral ...'

A Universal History of Infamy

This book includes the popular 'Streetcorner Man',
Borges's very first short story, and a selection of
brief tales in which human villainy becomes the victim of
fate, enchantment or its own perversity. Here, as well as
chronicling the lives of such famous villains as Billy the
Kid and the Tichborne Claimant, Borges perpetrates a
hoax or two – a technique for which he later won acclaim
– by inventing stories and ascribing them to other authors.

Labyrinths

The twenty-three stories in *Labyrinths* include Borges's
classic 'Tlön, Uqbar, Orbit Tertius', a new world where
external objects are whatever each person wants; and
'Pierre Menard', the story of the man who rewrote parts
of *Don Quixote* for the twentieth century in Cervantes's
words.

The ten essays reflect the extraordinary scope of Borges's
reading – the ancient literatures of Greece and China, the
medieval philosophers, Pascal, Shakespeare, Valéry, Shaw
and Wells – while the seven parables are unforgettable
exercises in the art of astonishment.

The Book of Sand

'These superb new stories . . . make marvellous thought-
provoking reading . . . Borges ponders, questions, examines
time, reality, thought, in extraordinary fashion in these
haunting, seemingly simple, very beautiful stories. A
major literary event' – *Publishers Weekly*

This volume also contains *The Gold of the Tigers:
Selected Later Poems*, in which understatement replaces
some of the glittering fireworks of Borges's poetry.